THE 4 Vs of
LEADERSHIP

THE 4 Vs of LEADERSHIP

Vision, Values, Value-added and Vitality

Peter Shaw CB

CAPSTONE

Other Wiley Editorial Offices

John Wiley & Sons Inc., 111 River Street, Hoboken, NJ 07030, USA
Jossey-Bass, 989 Market Street, San Francisco, CA 94103-1741, USA
Wiley-VCH Verlag GmbH, Boschstr. 12, D-69469 Weinheim, Germany
John Wiley & Sons Australia Ltd, 42 McDougall Street, Milton, Queensland 4064, Australia
John Wiley & Sons (Asia) Pte Ltd, 2 Clementi Loop #02-01, Jin Xing Distripark, Singapore 129809
John Wiley & Sons Canada Ltd, 22 Worcester Road, Etobicoke, Ontario, Canada M9W 1L1

A catalogue record for this book is available from the British Library and the Library of Congress.

ISBN-13: 978-1-84112-698-2   (PB)
ISBN-10: 1-84112-698-5   (PB)

Typeset in 11/13pt Photina by MCS Publishing Services Ltd, Salisbury, Wiltshire
Printed and bound in Great Britain by TJ International Ltd, Padstow, Cornwall

Substantial discounts on bulk quantities of Capstone Books are available to corporations,
professional associations and other organizations. For details telephone John Wiley & Sons
on (+44) 1243-770441, fax (+44) 1243 770571 or email corporatedevelopment@wiley.co.uk

Dedicated to
Frances and our children Graham, Ruth and Colin for their
wonderful support and special friendship.

Contents

Acknowledgements

The first time I worked one-to-one with individuals about the 4 Vs of vision, values, value-added and vitality was at a development centre for high-potential civil servants. I had focused, one-to-one conversations with six special people and challenged them to be clear about their next steps. It was a delight to work with them and to keep in touch since. I owe them a great deal for their encouragement to me: they were Anita Bharucha, Rod Clark, Charlie Massey, Jonathan Moor, Fiona Spencer and Pete Worrall. Their positive reaction to working with the 4 Vs set me off using this framework widely in the public, private and voluntary sectors, and it worked just as well with high-potential people in the City as it did with bishops.

As I developed my thinking on the 4 Vs I was particularly grateful for the time given to me by Ken Boston (the Chief Executive of the Qualifications and Curriculum Authority), John Dunford (the General Secretary of the Association of School and College Leaders), David Adelman (the Principal of Godalming Sixth Form College), Andrew Higginson (the Finance and Strategy Director for Tesco) and Suma Chakrabarti (the Permanent Secretary of the Department for International Development). I am grateful to them for allowing me to quote them directly in this book.

A wide range of people talked with me about the ideas in the book. Those who gave me special insights included Roger King, Sunil Patel, Delphine Rive, Mark Fisher, Andrew Hudson, Ann Wilmot, Jayne Colquhoun, Judith Hardy, Jill Kirby, Wendy Williams, Archie Hughes, Portia Ragnauth, Jane Frost, Una O'Brien, Paul Pugh and Andrew McDonald. They gave willingly of their time to talk through the relevance of the 4 Vs in different situations. My colleagues at Praesta Partners, especially Liz Walmsley, have always been ready to give me new insights.

Clare Sumner, Robin Linnecar and Ric Todd read an early draft of the text and provided lots of practical points. Their independent reflections were so important in building the final text. I am grateful to those who have been willing for their experiences to be incorporated into anonymised examples within the book.

I am also grateful to David Normington for writing the foreword. We were colleagues together over a ten-year period: he always brought practical good sense to every issue. I owe a great deal to colleagues with whom I worked in Government. When writing this book I kept in my mind the tough and focused advice I always received from Carol Hunter and Jeanette Pugh, who are two of the most impressive and supportive colleagues I worked with. They always brought clarity to any issue: I have tried to carry forward their practical good sense into this book.

Judy Smith has been a patient, thoughtful and long-suffering typist. She and I have never met! We have long conversations: I send my drafts to her in deepest Hampshire and they return as pristine chapters via email. My executive assistant, Claire Salkeld, has been outstanding in managing my diary so that interviews for the book could be squeezed into a busy coaching schedule.

Sally Smith has been a perceptive and thoughtful editor, brilliant at identifying key issues and enabling me to clarify next steps. The 4 Vs caught her imagination and I am grateful to her for taking forward this proposal with such commitment. Rebecca Dimery was a great help on practical editorial issues.

Finally, a huge debt of thanks is owed to my family. Frances has been wonderfully supportive. Our three children, Graham, Ruth and Colin, have always ensured that I didn't take my work too seriously, providing me with encouragement and lots of teasing. Without their good humour I would never have completed the book.

Peter Shaw

OTHER BOOKS BY PETER SHAW

Mirroring Jesus as Leader, Grove, 2004

Conversation Matters: How to Engage Effectively with One Another, Continuum, 2005

Finding your Future: The Second Time Around, Darton, Longman and Todd, publishing in Autumn 2006

Making Effective Use of Coaching, Capstone, publishing in Spring 2007

Foreword

I first spoke with Peter Shaw about his 4 Vs of leadership when I was preparing for my own next big career challenge as Permanent Secretary at the Home Office. Later, I read the final text just a few days before taking up the job. So I had an immediate point of reference for his ideas about how successful leaders combine clarity of vision, consistent values, the ability to add value, and fresh and renewable sources of vitality. As I read, I found myself constantly reassessing my own hopes, fears and ambitions in a new role against his thought-provoking, but always optimistic, template.

What I like about Peter's book is that, in contrast to so many treatises on leadership and management, he refuses to compartmentalise life into the personal and professional. He believes – rightly – that successful leaders bring a consistency of behaviour and relationships to different aspects of their lives and draw strength and inspiration from the personal to the professional and vice versa. He argues, where possible, for personal and organisational values to be aligned, something I strongly believe in. And in my favourite chapter – on vitality – he avoids stereotypical arguments about work/life balance and suggests that energy can be renewed and refreshed at work, at play, in voluntary work or spiritual renewal, or simply by doing nothing. He and I very much share a love of walking and fresh air as a means of clearing the head and finding refreshment and have often exchanged walking tips and ideas. But I came away from Chapter 5 with all kinds of new and additional insights.

The strength of Peter's book above all is that it is authentic. While it draws on a wide range of expertise and examples from others, it is also deeply rooted in his own experience: as a senior civil servant, as a reader in the Church of England, as a successful coach and as a much-sought-after communicator and teacher in leadership and management. He was a colleague of mine for over ten years and I know of few who so successfully blended their personal and family values with those of the public service or who brought such irrepressible vitality to his work. He writes at one point that successes should be captured and celebrated: don't just take the photographs, he says, display them. My office is festooned with Peter's photographs of successful leadership teams in which he and I have worked at the Department for Education and Skills, our former Department. A small example, but a real one, of him practising what he preaches.

At the end of his chapter on vitality, Peter writes briefly of his own change of career, moving into full-time leadership coaching after thirty years in Government. He describes his initial apprehension despite the fact that he was about to do something he had always wanted to do: but in a short time 'moving on for me created a whole new energy'. This book is a wonderful affirmation of how successful his transition has been. It will bring wisdom and stimulation to people at all stages of their lives and careers: to those who are moving up or moving on at work or are seeking new challenges in their personal lives, or are looking for new sources of ideas and energy.

David Normington
Permanent Secretary, Home Office

Chapter 1:

The Journey Ahead

True hope is swift and flies with swallow's wings; Kings it makes gods, and meaner creatures kings.

William Shakespeare

Focusing on the 4 Vs of **vision**, **values**, **value-added** and **vitality** can reshape your life. The 4 Vs are the corners of a diamond which, taken together, are the essential ingredients of effective leadership. In combination, the diamond they create will light up both your work and personal life.

This framework has worked well with leaders across the private, public and voluntary sectors. Its application knows no boundaries. The 4 Vs have resonated strongly with leaders in very different worlds because:

- they are easy to remember,
- they are dynamic,
- they link together personal and organisation priorities,
- they are relevant at any age or stage in your career, and
- they provide a framework for major decisions about priorities.

The 4 Vs will help you:

- become more focused in your personal **vision** and potentially equip you for more senior posts,
- become more explicit in defining your **values** and in reassessing your life priorities against those values,
- become clearer about your **value-added** contributions and enable you to delegate more effectively, and

- reassess how you use your energy, enabling you to spend more time on the activities that are most important to you – which will raise your **vitality**.

What has caught the imagination is that the 4 Vs cut right across personal, work, family and community priorities. Working through the implications of the 4 Vs has covered economic, physical, emotional and spiritual wellbeing. It has provided individuals with the framework and the space to make new decisions about their future.

The 4 Vs have not imposed an external philosophy or world view. Their purpose is not to advocate a particular set of values, or vision, or way of adding value, or sources of vitality. They have enabled individuals to define where they stand more clearly and the next steps on their journey, and have provided an equally powerful framework for people from Christian, Hindu, Jewish, Humanist, Muslim or Sikh heritages and for those of no strong religious or cultural background.

My vision for you

Be ready to:

- clarify your personal vision,
- live your values,
- focus your value-added, and
- grow your sources of vitality.

You should be open-minded and honest with yourself. Working through the 4 Vs could lead to radical next steps. It could be a dangerous and life-changing exercise. Your starting points might be:

- Does your personal vision need to change? Maybe it is too vague or too rigid.
- Do your values influence you in the ways you want?
- Does your value-added in different spheres need to change?
- Is your vitality a bit squashed or randomly directed?

Working through the 4 Vs could lead to a whole range of different next steps. It could be:

- Taking forward specific aspects of your personal **vision**.
- Focusing on two or three key **values** and looking at how you apply them across each aspect of your life.

- Being much more precise about defining your own **value-added** and what difference you want to make in a range of different contexts.
- Being much more self-aware about the reasons for your own levels of **vitality** and how you are going to grow specific sources of vitality – which might sometimes involve activity and sometimes the complete absence of activity.

In writing this book my hope for you is that:

Vision. Your vision will become clearer. It might be a specific vision in terms of your work or your community. There will be a coherence in your vision of who you are and who you want to be that links each aspect of your life: it will be a dynamic vision that is evolving with you enabling constructive changes to happen in different spheres of your life while recognising your responsibilities.

Values. Your values will be consistent across each aspect of your life. You will understand where your values come from and why they are such a core part of you. You will intend to take forward your values strongly in the way you live in community with others. You will be looking at all your decisions in relation to your values.

Value-added. You will have thought very hard about where you want to add value. You will be rehearsing and practising in areas where you want to strengthen your capacity to do so. You will not be daunted for long by setbacks but will be developing the resilience to maintain your value-added whatever the pressures.

Vitality. You will have taken a fresh look at your sources of energy. You will be experimenting with different ways of ensuring freshness and joy in your life. You will have moved on from the notion of rigid concepts of work/life balance to testing how each activity is sapping you or re-energising you. You will be viewing time in a very different sort of way and will not be ruled by the clock; instead you will be strongly influenced in your use of time by how you can influence others for good in the most constructive way.

Why these 4 Vs?

To move forward in any area of our lives depends on linking together vision, values, value-added and vitality. Why?

Vision. This enables us to be very clear who we want to be. What is the essential Wendy-ness, Mark-ness or Mohammed-ness? What is the coherence of our vision of ourselves that brings together our work, community and home personalities into one coherent person?

Values. What are the values that drive us? Do we understand where they came from and how they are changing? How can we harness our values to help our own fulfilment and the wellbeing of those around us? How do we ensure our values are our biggest asset and not our worst liability?

Value-added. What are our strengths? How can we develop them and use them to the best effect? What are we less good at? How can we develop skills in those areas? How can we become more confident in adding value in a wider range of different situations? How can we add value in all our interactions with different people so that they are enlightened and encouraged?

Vitality. What is at the heart of what gives us energy? Can we grow that source of energy? Can we take it into different areas of our lives? What is the interlink between what gives us energy at home and in the community? How can those sources of energy flow back into our work situations? What part does stillness play in nurturing our sources of energy?

What next?

This book is predicated on the assumption that you want to be even more self-aware. It will stretch you in terms of your being objective and tough on yourself. It will equally stretch you in terms of how you care for yourself and others, and enable those around you to grow in understanding. You will see your past successes and failures in a new light.

There is a substantive chapter on each of the 4 Vs which can be read separately or consecutively as a sequence. Each one concludes with a set of questions for reflection either individually or in groups. A number of individuals have agreed to their perspectives being included in the book. Many of them feature in each of the chapters. Some of them talk from the wealth of their experience about the importance of vision, values, value-added and vitality. These include Ken Boston (the chief executive of a government agency), Andrew Higginson (a board member of Tesco),

David Adelman (the principal of a sixth form college), John Dunford (the general secretary of a professional association) and Suma Chakrabarti (a Permanent Secretary and head of a government department). Other perspectives come from individuals who have used the 4 Vs as a framework for their own development. All these stories illustrate the wide applicability of the 4 Vs.

The book encourages you to take forward your conclusions through a balance of courage and calmness, through a careful reflection of what is success and through reflection about next steps. Only read it if you are willing to challenge yourself. Be open to change. Be ready to be surprised. Above all grow the qualities and values that are most important to you. Let the 4 Vs provide the four corners of the diamond which will sparkle in even the darkest night or the brightest day.

Chapter 2:

Vision

Where there is no vision, the people perish.

Proverbs, Chapter 29

When you are fully engaged in day-to-day life, talking of a vision for the future can seem trite or self-indulgent; it can appear to be ducking your current responsibilities. We can dismiss thinking about the future because it distracts us from addressing current problems. But the opposite can be true: thinking in a constructive way about the future puts the present into a context. It helps give us a sense of perspective and purpose. Spending some time looking at our vision for the future is one of the most healthy things we can do. We need to dream dreams but not become a servant to our dreams.

The definition of vision I am using is 'having a clear perspective about who you are and what you aim to be doing in the future'. This definition does not include a particular timescale: that will depend on individual circumstances. It is a personal vision, although there will be interactions between the personal dimension and the corporate vision of any organisation in which you have a significant role.

The themes of this chapter include:

- Starting with an accurate self-assessment.
- Building your personal vision for the future.
- The interlinking between a personal vision and a corporate vision.
- Living your vision.
- Accepting that your personal vision will need to change.

Make an honest self-assessment

The starting point has to be where you are now and an honest self-assessment, looking backwards and then forwards. As you look back what are:

- Your greatest joys and pleasures?
- Your greatest successes?
- Your biggest failures?
- How have these joys, successes and failures moulded you?

This process may sound indulgent but is essential in building up an accurate picture of who you are. It is important to be just as honest about failures as successes, through trying to understand why they happened and what learning has been involved. For each major success it is worth reflecting on:

- What did you do that made the difference?
- Who helped you to focus your learning?
- How did the success itself develop your own competences and courage?

For each major failure:

- What did you learn from it?
- Did it teach you that you were going down a blind alley?
- Did you learn some specific skills in terms of effective preparation?
- Was there learning in terms of how you react emotionally to failure?
- Was the failure caused partly because there was a sense of anxiety that disrupted your rhythm?

An objective look at your successes and failures provides a very sound platform for understanding the present and looking to the future. In terms of your present position:

- Are you comfortable that you put your time and energy now where you want it to be in the future?
- Is there a discontinuity between the current focus of your efforts and your ideal?
- Are you bogged down in certain aspects of your life, seeing no light at the end of the tunnel?
- Are there moments when it feels overwhelming or times when there is a hint of panic?

Look five years on

Look ahead five years and reflect on:

- What are the **joys** that are going to be most important to you? What, for you, will **success** be? It could be large or small in other people's eyes. What matters is what is a realistic aspiration of success for you.
- What are the **failures** you are most concerned about? What are the failures that may well happen which you would be comfortable learning through?

Looking at your **joys** first, what are they about?

- Seeing the outcomes of your work, e.g. children learning, a new hospital built, a more efficient accounting system?
- Time with those personally closest to you?
- How big a place has shared pleasures with your family?
- How much is about intellectual, physical, emotional or spiritual growth and awareness?

In terms of your **successes** how much of the pleasure comes from:

- Your own self-fulfilment?
- The financial security you are able to bring to others?
- The impact for good you are able to have on others?
- Fulfilling the expectations of others, like your family or your boss?

In terms of your **failures** what will give you greatest satisfaction? Is it:

- You avoided even bigger failures?
- The learning that has come through trying and failing?
- The satisfaction that only by being brave enough to take risks has there been learning through failure?

Building on your strengths

When you visualise who you are five years on, it is crucial that you build on who you are now and do not try and turn yourself completely inside out. The starting point has to be an accurate self-perception of your strengths and weaknesses. The key questions become:

- How can you develop your strengths in a way that is realistic and bold at the same time?
- How can your strengths be moulded into something quite profound?
- What are the step changes needed to use your strengths ever more effectively?
- What is the strength that most surprises you but would give you the greatest pleasure to grow and develop?

Often our self-perception of our strengths is partial. Trusted friends and colleagues can give accurate feedback, although the closest friends may not be entirely objective. Some of the most dispassionate advice might come from your spouse or partner. Those colleagues you trust at work or in the community can be an invaluable source of objective assessment. It is not an indulgence to ask for their perceptions, it is an abdication of duty to yourself not to ask. When you ask them about your failings, encourage them to be objective and precise; ask them to be frank and encouraging at the same time. Watch out if you react defensively to their comments and try to be utterly objective yourself.

A crucial starting point is being utterly philosophic about future failings. Looking five years ahead, how will you view your failures? Is it that you:

- Did not have the right opportunities?
- Were preoccupied with other things?
- Were not that bothered?
- Gave up?
- Could see progress you had made but recognised that it was only partial?

With top teams I sometimes do an exercise of asking each member of the team to do a self-assessment and then an assessment of each of their colleagues, identifying the three greatest strengths and three areas for development. We then share these assessments openly so that each member of the senior team sees their own assessment alongside the assessment by their colleagues. I ask each member of the group to reflect individually on the messages this gives and then to reflect back some observations to the wider group. I dwell at considerable length on the strengths as there is a tendency for people to want to rush straight into the areas for development without celebrating and internalising their strengths. Building on strengths is such an important part of defining your own vision for the future. Equally important is the honesty of looking at areas for development based on the views of trusted others.

Sit yourself in the shoes of the person who you will be in five years time and ask these questions:

- What are the strengths I have grown? List the top three.
- What are the joys I am experiencing in an even stronger way?
- How am I now coping with tough decisions?
- Have I got the balance of my use of energy better sorted?
- Has there been learning through mistakes?
- Can I identify the failures I have had and what my learning has been through them?
- Are my work, community and family interests in balance?

Once you have been utterly objective about how you want to be five years on, what is it you now need to work on so that you can change in the way you want to? Is it about:

- Your own self-perception?
- The way you use your energy and time?
- The support you allow yourself to receive from others?
- Your willingness to experiment and learn?
- Your focus in searching after what you think is important?
- Embracing the passions that are most important to you? That could be professional success, enabling your children to grow up, making music, taking a leading role in your community or faith group ...

What you then decide to change may be about:

- Your attitude to yourself.
- Your approach and openness to others.
- Your priorities in terms of your intellectual, physical, emotional and spiritual energies.
- Your willingness to be influenced by people you trust.

Keep looking ahead

You cannot create a vision for yourself for five years ahead in a vacuum. We can think about different situations five years on and imagine ourselves in those situations. What would it be like to be a head of department, a partner, a senior manager or a foreman? We can do this through a number of steps:

- At a basic level we can imagine where we are sitting or what we are wearing.
- We can reflect on the issues we will be involved in and the type of decisions we will be making.
- We can imagine the joys and the frustrations of that role.

Defining the role as precisely as we can will enable us to decide whether that is where we want to be. When I work with people who are thinking about what sort of job they might be doing in five years time, I encourage them to sit explicitly in different roles. I encourage them to think of what they are seeing, hearing, touching and smelling. Key elements are:

- Being utterly objective about what they are doing and whether they are making a difference or not.
- Being very clear emotionally about whether the role is giving them pleasure.
- Being clear on whether the role is physically energising.
- Reflecting on whether the role is worthwhile in terms of fulfilling their personal aspirations.

Sometimes visioning cannot be about a precise picture of where you might be and what you are doing. Sometimes being open to a vision for the future is being willing to set off on a journey. The vision is about opening up doors and seeing what happens: it is about creating the freedoms and flexibilities that will allow other people to blossom and grow. Part of this is about giving yourself time to reflect and explore different avenues – not easy to do in a society of immediate gratification and when the expectation is to strive for quick promotion and recognition.

John Dunford, the General Secretary of the Association of School and College Leaders (formerly the Secondary Heads' Association), talks of the value of having a vision for change when he was a head teacher of a school in Durham. For example, he ensured international exchanges for pupils with schools in Russia and Japan and initiated a programme of having an artist in residence regularly. He regarded these themes as 'creating opportunities for success'. On the one hand he had a clear vision for change, on the other, through recognising individual teachers and through giving them seed-corn funds for different projects, he was 'pouring on water and watching other people's ideas grow'.

His vision was to enable his staff to grow their own vision. He encouraged them to be innovative and unleash their own creativity. His initial philosophy as head teacher was 'creating opportunities for success' which provided a vision to which others could respond. He says that his motto now would be more on the lines of 'creating opportunities and then making sure things happen', as there must be a strong drive from the leader not just to raise expectations and raise the sights of others but also to make sure that the vision is strong enough so that every youngster develops to their full potential.

John's motto of 'creating opportunities and then making sure things happen' is a necessary part of an effective vision. In too many organisations the assumption is that most ideas never turn into reality. Having both a clear vision and the means of enabling outcomes that deliver the vision is the sometimes elusive but necessary combination.

At the heart of a dynamic vision is the willingness to expand horizons. At a basic level this freshness comes from balancing the routine things you enjoy with new experiences: it means both. Does it always have to be chips, why not duchesse potatoes? It means savouring and enjoying the richness of what makes you feel comfortable – hot chocolate, the old slippers, the Beethoven or Beatles music – and at the same time experimenting with new places, new people, new thought processes and not being afraid to make mistakes.

It might mean reflecting each week on what you have really enjoyed doing and what you have experimented with. How have those successful experiments built a new dimension into your vision for the future? Perhaps it has only been in a small way, but when you are continually learning your vision for the future will keep changing.

Clarifying the personal vision of who you want to be can have a rapid impact on how you come over to different people. This illustration is of Janet, for whom there were marked changes over a one year period. She held a senior post within a national organisation where she led on performance management and worked directly to the Chief Executive. Janet is quite small and in our first conversation was diffident and lacking in confidence. There were times in meetings when she said she felt foolish and ill-prepared. She clearly had the ability and wisdom to do her job really well. She sometimes didn't press her point as much as she wanted to and she was very deferential to senior managers. In our first meeting it was clear that her confidence levels were holding her back.

A year later it was a different story. She spoke more confidently and firmly. Her eye contact was much better; she sat in her chair with much greater authority. She had been contributing effectively with board members, and she was challenging the CEO: he was amused by her ability to organise his agenda very skilfully. He was responding to this well and encouraging her to think about her next post at a more senior level.

I asked her what had made the difference over the year. She said it was a combination of factors: she had pushed her points more boldly and people had responded well. She used her considerable intellect and wisdom more forcefully in influencing discussions. She had taught herself to ask questions in a much firmer way and to be persistent in following up points clearly when the answers were vague.

Janet says that when she is nervous she deliberately breathes deeply and places both feet firmly on the ground. She holds firmly on to the vision of the changed organisation she is helping to create and is now firmer and more challenging. The vision for herself still has further to go and she wants to operate more comfortably at a senior level. She has been doing a personal performance role and now wants to develop her contribution into a more rounded performance as a senior leader, building on the management skills she developed in an earlier post.

Janet had deliberately moved every couple of years from one demanding job to another. It would now be very easy to stay put but it was right to move on. She wanted to manage a larger entity. We talked about her vision for her next role and why she would choose a particular job. Her initial test was that she could do the job itself and we discussed whether that was the right criteria. She had moved from demanding job to demanding job. Was she setting her sights too low if the job was one that she was confident she could do from the start? She acknowledged that she didn't always stretch herself as much as she could. We talked about two other criteria:

- Would the job engage her interest (both intellectually and emotionally) and give her joy?
- Would it develop her skills and understanding?

As she thought about the next job it was clear that the interest test was very important. Where could she make the biggest difference? She wanted to stay within the same family of organisations, because she was not bored by the work and thought the organisation had a crucial future role. The passion was there to do a major leadership role within the organisation in the future.

Janet was not now feeling foolish or ill-prepared. She had grown significantly during the year. Talking to her, it was as if she had grown in stature physically. She certainly had in terms of wisdom and authority.

Relevant questions are:

- How quickly do you think that a clearer vision of who you are will affect your demeanour and impact on others?
- How strong is your wish to impact differently on others within a reasonably short period of time?

Let your vision for yourself be bold and realistic

A clear vision is a strong driver. When I walked the 109 miles across England from Arnside in Cumbria to Saltburn in Cleveland I had a clear picture of striding down Saltburn Pier nine days after leaving Arnside Pier. That vision was a very strong driver through the nine days, as I walked over the Pennines and through the Yorkshire Dales. It was all the more powerful because there was a clear picture in my mind of the metal railings of Saltburn Pier, the sandy beach and the sea air.

What follows are examples of individuals who have developed a bold and realistic vision of the impact they want to have.

Ken Boston is Chief Executive of the Qualifications and Curriculum Authority in London, having held various chief executive posts within the Australian education system. His advice is 'dream dreams but recognise that you will have more hallucinations than visions'. He argues that when you have a dream you should exercise the discipline of planning how you are going to get there, who you need to get onside and what resources you need. How, in precise terms, are you going to make it happen? Only then do you have a vision; until these key issues are sorted out you are just hallucinating. Unless the strategy and resources are all assembled the dream will never happen. Make sure that the vision is about tactics as well as goals. Ken Boston is an expert in painting a visionary picture for the future. He will often do this in speeches in order to set a clear direction. For vision to work there has to be a focus on the linked aspects of the ultimate goal, the strategy and the tactics. Keeping the vision dynamic means reflecting each weekend about what has been achieved over the previous week and where this is leading for the future in terms of the overall vision.

Richard recently became the Chief Executive of a major international organisation. We talked about how important was it for him to have a vision for the future of the organisation. He said he knew what outcomes he wanted but he was always watching the context. He was holding himself back from rushing in. His advice to himself was 'If you see a hole don't feel you have got to fill it. Don't assume your perspective is the right one. Keep listening. Watch the fact that to go quickly can be to go slowly. Keep the pace right. Keep a clear focus on what aspects of the vision are most important and ensure a balance between the strategic and the tactical'.

That combination of stretching the boundaries and realism is at the heart of a vision that works: a vision that embraces goals, strategy and tactics, and ensures effective partnerships and common interest. Looking forward at a clear vision need not be a delusion. If people are moving into a new situation I often encourage them to think about how they want to reinvent themselves in a new role:

- What are the strengths they want to build on?
- What sort of impact do they want to have on people they are meeting?
- What priorities do they want to set out?
- What type of energy levels are they wanting to show?

I often ask them to reflect on what adjectives they want the people they will shortly be meeting to use to describe them. When an individual articulates these words they begin to visualise whether they are comfortable with them or not. If one of the words is 'supportive', we work through what that word means and how they are going to display that attribute.

Alex had a reputation as a tough, uncompromising negotiator who never listened. He got results but at a huge cost. He eventually alienated so many people that he was sidelined and had little credibility. He decided he wanted to rebuild his reputation as a good listener and visualised what being a good listener meant in terms of:

- visiting his colleagues,
- maintaining strong eye contact,
- repeating back to them key points they had made,
- allowing them to complete their points, and
- not rubbing it in when he was right.

Applying these practical steps made a worthwhile difference. He still got the results he wanted on big issues, and carried people with him much more effectively.

Another way of creating a future vision is to reflect on what next year's model is and how it differs from this year's model. Is next year's model:

- Faster or does it have a better cruise control?
- Does it turn round corners more smoothly?
- Does it anticipate changes in the road more easily?
- How comfortable is it to be a passenger alongside the driver?
- How easily, in next year's model, can you see what is coming up behind?

If you think in a visual way, then imagining yourself as next year's model can provide a new way of thinking about how you want to reinvent yourself next year. Is it some reshaping you need or a radical overhaul?

Sustain a vision of success in your work which reinforces personal priorities

Consistency between priority areas is crucial for our wellbeing. There will inevitably be a tension sometimes between different aspects of your priorities in different areas of your life, but striving for a consistency of vision is essential for your own fulfilment and peace of mind. It certainly helps if a vision of success at work reinforces personal priorities. Often this vision of the nature of success will evolve over time.

As an example, David Adelman, the principal of a sixth form college, talks of his vision as a senior manager as being rooted in early experiences outside management. He said he spent fourteen years as a rather 'rebellious' and outspoken classroom teacher of history before becoming a senior manager. This experience was formative in that it gave him an insight into what classroom teachers need in terms of support and understanding from management. In his experience as a classroom teacher he felt that many teachers viewed senior managers as the 'enemy' and, likewise, many senior managers viewed teachers in the same light. He eventually came to realise that this 'us' and 'them' mentality was corrosive, undermining the sense of a being part of a single community with a common purpose which is the hallmark of a successful organisation. He developed the strong conviction that it is the responsibility of senior managers to try to ensure that the educational purpose of institutions is not corrupted by mutual suspicion and conflict between managers and teachers. However, David was at first determined not to 'turn traitor' and become a manager himself.

This uncompromising outlook changed for a number of reasons. Firstly, as he says himself, he 'grew up'. Secondly, the failure of Communism – symbolised by the fall of the Berlin Wall in 1989 and the success of Thatcherism with people from all walks of life – brought the point home that a simple left/right perspective was no longer viable. Thirdly, a young vice-principal at the college at which he worked proved to be a powerful role model, demonstrating that it was possible for a senior manager to be both effective and empathic, practical and progressive.

David then began applying for promotion and moved in a matter of six years from being a teacher to a principal, serving as a director of curriculum and a deputy principal along the way. As a senior leader he has retained a strong commitment to a better and more equal society and continues to see education as a powerful force for good, just as he did as a younger man. Indeed, he sees it as important that people with progressive or left-wing views become leaders in the public or private sectors in order to ensure that organisations have a clear moral purpose. At the same time he now recognises that in a complex world you have to be willing to make compromises; you have to be pragmatic but without losing sight of the original ideals and beliefs which motivated you to go into education in the first place. He feels that pragmatism without idealism is soulless, idealism without pragmatism is reckless. He still teaches in the classroom whenever he can, believing that you have to lead from the front: head teachers should teach if they are going to manage and motivate teachers. He delivers outstanding leadership of a successful college.

Each of us can be faced with dilemmas about whether our vision of success at work is consistent with our personal priorities. The key steps are:

- Being absolutely honest about the dilemmas.
- Recognising the extent to which we are on a journey in terms of changes in our personal priorities.
- Trying to measure quite precisely the consequences when our work and personal priorities are in conflict in terms of our use of time and energy.
- Identifying the two or three top personal priorities and the two or three top work priorities in terms of our vision for the future and looking hard at how they can be interrelated.
- Being clear about what is the most productive and least harmful way of bringing those priorities into line.

Be reflective about what fulfilment is

Fulfilment is never easy to define: it is a personal and changing picture. There is always another hill to climb. It must be right both to have fixed points and to be flexible. When our children were aged 7, 9 and 11 we walked up the three highest peaks in Scotland, Wales and England (Ben Nevis, Snowdon and Scafell Pike). This gave the children a strong sense of fulfilment: it was a fulfilment that was clear and planned. My eldest son has done a lot of detached youth work. In this world you cannot plan in advance; it depends who you meet and what their needs are. The greatest fulfilment for him came through unexpected conversations.

Part of fulfilment is setting out a prospectus in advance. Clarity about outcomes is a powerful driver, be it about the delivery of a teaching programme or lecture, the operations to be performed, or the holes to be dug. Part of fulfilment is retrospective: looking back over a day can mean identifying moments of success which had not been planned for. It could be the breakthrough in a meeting, the new understanding about a particular individual or situation, or the words of thanks that have come from someone you had encouraged or stretched.

The vision dimension of fulfilment is both about focused preplanning and about being open to unexpected moments of fulfilment. Taking the time to absorb and embrace those moments of fulfilment is so important: it is by internalising them that we make ever stronger our own vision of who we are and who we want to be.

Striving for fulfilment can make us too single-minded and blinker us to the reality of the world around us. Fulfilment is about the climbing of mountains, but it is also about creating times of calm, a calmness which is partly to enable us to enjoy and internalise those moments of fulfilment. As we vision our future, keeping a focus on moments of calm is valuable: if we can create times when we are calm then we will be much more at peace with ourselves. The times of calmness could, for example, be when walking, cooking, reading, listening to music, fishing or doing aerobics. The best sort of calmness for you, whatever it is, is a crucial ingredient of your future vision. We leave out that dimension of our future at our peril.

Who are your role models?

Role models are powerful and dangerous pictures. They are essential in terms of defining the sort of person we want to be. They are dangerous in terms of trying to ape somebody else and not make our distinctive contribution. If someone tries to imitate the surface behaviour and not embed substantive learning it can lead to a bit of a sham.

Imagining yourself as someone else can provide a very powerful role model. The thought process can be as follows:

- Which two or three people do you particularly admire?
- What is it about the way they react in particular situations that you would like to emulate – maybe it is their capacity to be reflective or decisive?
- Observe how they react and note their sense of timing, their use of words and the thought process they go through.
- Identify two or three things that you want to embrace and be clear how you are going to practise them.
- Find opportunities in which to use the approaches and techniques which you want to take on.
- Be equally clear what aspects of the individual's approach you are not comfortable with and be quite explicit that you are not going to take on that aspect of their approach, for no one is perfect. Being particularly clear about what aspects you are not going to emulate means you are differentiating in an objective way.

Sometimes we can be our most powerful role model. At the centre of developing your own vision is clarity about who you are. What are the characteristics which most sum you up? What topics of thought or conversation give you greatest energy? What sort of conversation enlivens you? As you define the key characteristics of who you are, you are defining your own role model in terms of the essential features of your future vision. What is the essential element that makes us ourselves? What is the essential Mark-ness, Wendy-ness or Mohammed-ness? This is not to abdicate the responsibility to grow and change. It is saying that there are certain core things about your emotions and reactions that you enjoy and enliven you, and that these need to be part of the core as you move on.

What are your leadership priorities?

Thinking yourself into the shoes of different leaders will force you to reflect on what is your preferred style of leadership. It will make you reflect on the balance between leadership from the front or leadership that serves others. Some commentators have focused on the importance of an up-front vision. John Kotter, from the Harvard Business School, puts a strong focus on the importance of vision, with successful leaders in both the private and public sector displaying a clear vision, a strategy for achieving that vision, a cooperative network of resources to help them deliver the vision and a group of highly motivated people willing to implement it.

On the other hand the servant theme is strong in many commentators. Stephen Covey, probably the best known of all the writers on leadership, talks of the leader who serves, with a spirit of service being essential for the leader in any sphere. He links this to the main source of personal change coming from pain, with pain creating the motivation and humility to change.

Jim Collins, in *From Good to Great*, tells stories of successful businesses around the western world. He sums up successful leaders in the book as demonstrating a combination of unwavering resolve and compelling modesty, a phrase that brings together both a clarity of vision and servanthood as part of vision.

In my book *Mirroring Jesus as Leader* I summarise six strands of leadership in terms of the leader as visionary, servant, teacher, coach, radical and healer with the best of leaders embedding all these different strands. Each leader will find some of these characteristics more difficult than others. My thesis is that the missing virtue in much leadership writing and leadership practice is the leader as healer.

If a leader focuses on healing, both amongst peers and within the organisation more generally, the impact can be huge. The effective healing leader does it quietly and unassumingly: it is the act of doing it in a self-effacing way that ensures its effectiveness. The healing role raises big issues about what generosity of spirit means and how often you forgive. Part of developing your own style of leadership is reinforcing that delicate balance between the six strands of visionary, servant, teacher, coach, radical and healer.

As you reflect on role models reflect on that balance between:

- leading from the front in terms of taking direct action, and enabling and serving others to fulfil their own visions, and
- providing a healing role in building and renewing relationships.

The interrelation between corporate and personal vision

Many organisations of which we are part will have corporate vision statements. Sometimes they are ignored, sometimes they can be a powerful touchstone. Corporate visions may affect us in different ways:

- Are we comfortable working within a particular corporate vision?
- Do we have enough scope to develop our own personal vision within that corporate framework?
- Do we have the opportunity to influence the corporate vision?

This section looks at:

- Why organisations have corporate visions.
- The potential relevance of corporate visions for individuals.

In *Change: How to Adapt and Transform a Business*, N. Anand describes a corporate vision as

> ' ... an idea of the future that acts as a focal point for all change efforts. Vision is about having a picture of the changed organisation as it will be when change has been successful: a sense of "how it looks when it works". To be an effective tool, vision has to have substance. It should not be a management fantasy, slogan or platitude. Good visions function as useful guides and inspiration to those who have to make changes happen. They help to cut through doubts and details by getting to the heart of whether any particular project or action is the right one – does it contribute to realising our vision? If not, should it proceed?'

Anand emphasises that a good vision is clear and intelligible to everyone in the organisation, giving them a common goal to work towards. Just as the need for change needs to be articulated in a common language, a vision needs to express the desired future in a universally comprehensive way.

The management thinker John Kotter sees clear vision as a crucial part of ensuring effective change. His themes are:

- increase urgency,
- build the guiding team,
- get the vision right,
- communicate for buy-in,
- empowering action,
- create short term wins,

- do not let up, and
- make change stick through striving for sustainability.

In communicating a vision of change, he focuses on: keep it simple, repeat and reinforce the message, do not act in a way that is inconsistent with the vision, address any perceived inconsistencies between vision and action, and make communication two-way.

These insights are relevant both where:

- we are helping to create a vision for an organisation,
- we are taking forward a corporate vision within our part of the organisation, and
- we are interrelating a corporate and personal vision so that we are able to contribute within an organisation with energy and integrity.

If an organisation presents its corporate vision purely as a top-down approach it can produce alienation. Where it works best there is a symmetry between the vision of individuals and that of the overall organisation.

AstraZeneca has used the following global leadership capabilities.

Provides clarity about strategic direction	Develops a vision of the future, answering the questions 'why' and 'what'
Ensures commitment	Builds commitment for the shared vision and creates a climate of empowerment
Focuses on delivery	Takes responsibility for decisions, results and creating a challenging, action-orientated environment
Builds relationships	Works from the premise that nothing important gets done alone – friendliness with a purpose
Develops people	Builds employee capability to improve current and future productivity
Demonstrations personal conviction	Communicates belief and commitment through energy and feelings

The word vision comes in both of the first two indents. The first is about developing a vision of the future asking questions of 'why' and 'what'; the second is about creating a climate of empowerment. This framework encourages an individual to develop their distinctive contribution within a shared vision.

The Environment Agency has set out a clear statement of its vision, as in the box below.

Environment Agency Vision

The Environment Agency's vision is of a rich, healthy and diverse environment for present and future generations.

We want people to have peace of mind, knowing that they live in a clean and safe environment, rich in wildlife and natural diversity – one they can enjoy to the full, but feel motivated to care for.

Achieving Our Vision Means ...

A better quality of life
People will know that they live in a healthier environment, richer in wildlife and natural diversity, an environment they can enjoy and feel motivated to care for.

An enhanced environment for wildlife
Wildlife will thrive in urban and rural areas. Habitats will improve for the benefits of all species. Everyone will understand the importance of safeguarding biodiversity.

Cleaner air for everyone
The emission of chemical pollutants into the atmosphere will decline greatly and will be below the level at which they can do significant harm.

Improved and protected inland and coastal waters
Our rivers, lakes and waters will be far cleaner. They will sustain diverse and healthy ecosystems, water sports and recreation.

Restored, protected land with healthier soils
Our land and soils will be exposed far less to pollutants. They will

support a wide range of uses, including production of healthy, nutritious food and other crops without damaging wildlife.

A greener business world
Industry and businesses will value the assets of a rich and diverse natural environment. In the process, they will: reap the benefits of sustainable business practices, improve competitiveness and value, and secure trust in the wider community.

Wiser, sustainable use of natural resources
All organisations and individuals will minimise the waste they produce. They will reuse and recycle materials far more intensively and use energy and materials more efficiently.

Limiting and adapting to climate change
Drastic cuts will be made in the emission of 'greenhouse gases' such as carbon dioxide. Society as a whole will be prepared for probable changes in our climate.

Reducing flood risk
Flood warnings and sustainable defences will continue to minimise injury, damage and distress from flooding. The role of wetlands in reducing flood risk will be recognised and the environmental benefits from nature floods will be maximised.

The Environment Agency vision provides a very clear framework for individuals in terms of recognising their role in the organisation. It provides clarity about the overall direction of the organisation and a confidence for the employee in taking forward their responsibilities.

This particular vision includes visual words and is purposeful. A quick read of these words leaves pictures in your mind about wildlife, a greener business world and a better use of natural resources. The simple initial phrase about a 'rich, healthy and diverse environment' has a clear focus. Because the vision statement is dynamic and visual it provides a good basis for individuals to see where their own personal vision fits in with the organisation's vision. The dynamic and visual element of this corporate vision is equally relevant for a personal vision.

The Highways Agency is responsible for all the motorways and trunk roads in England and Wales. It set out in 'Customers First' an overall aim of 'safe roads, reliable journeys, informed travellers' and a vision for the next five years. The key strands of that vision are:

- We put our customers first in everything we do, understanding and responding to their needs.
- We are a progressive, adaptable organisation with the skills and capabilities we need to deliver an effective and efficient service to customers and provide the best possible value for money.
- Our customers and those who work on our roads will enjoy improved safety.
- Our customers will enjoy more reliable journeys on a network that is sustainable, strikes the best environmental balance and provides best value.
- Our customers will have easy access to reliable, accurate information when and where they need it to help them better plan and complete their journeys.

The Highways Agency Chief Executive, Archie Robertson, has put considerable personal efforts into describing and living the different element of the vision. His message to all his staff has been clear: 'We shall all have a part to play in delivering the visions in "Customers First". Your contribution is critical to our success'.

The key strands of learning from the Highways Agency experience are the importance of:

- the personal and visible commitment of the Chief Executive,
- the clarity of different strands of the vision,
- a clear commitment about what the leadership in an organisation is going to do and how the world will be different,
- the importance of engagement with staff in developing and living a vision, and
- a clear link to values (see Chapter 3).

Peter Senge, in *The Fifth Discipline Fieldbook* written with other colleagues, talks of corporate planning with five steps:

- a personal vision,
- shared vision,
- a map of current reality,
- how we close the gap, and
- choice and implementation.

The book's theme is that a key starting point is the personal vision of individuals within an organisation. The writers advocate giving individuals 'an opportunity to talk about their personal vision of their life as a whole. What do they want to see for themselves in the future? With that as a starting point, how can their vision for the organisation reflect and amplify their individual vision?' Out of this process evolves a shared vision, then a test against reality before hard decisions are taken about the inter-relationship between personal and corporate vision.

The classic model is to start with a vision for an organisation, albeit with consultation, and then move to personal vision for individuals. The thinking of Peter Senge and his colleagues is focusing on a rather different approach of using personal vision as a starting point and then looking at the interaction with the organisational vision. This approach only works if there is a reasonable alignment in the first place, or the possibility of significant realignment.

If you are leading a team and there *is* a reasonable alignment in the first place, then it can be worthwhile to ask team members to set out clearly their own vision for their personal contributions and then see what this adds up to as a whole and whether the overall vision for the organisation can be modified to take account of personal preferences. If this can be done effectively for a team it can have a very motivating outcome.

Individuals may choose to work in specific areas because of a strong personal vision. They may have a vision about the difference they would like to make as a teacher or nurse. There may be a natural synergy between their personal vision and the organisational vision: but the tension may be particularly acute in these sectors when the individual teacher or nurse may not share the perspective of the government of the day or the relevant funding body. There is always going to be some tension between an individual's personal vision and an organisational vision but living with that tension is necessary and can be creative.

Build partnerships through a sustaining vision

It is fine to have a clear personal vision, but in isolation it is unlikely to succeed. A vision as a family only happens if each member of the family shares that vision. For an organisation, a vision only happens if there is buy-in from key people. There is no point in having a vision to fulfil a particular role in a community if you do not have support. Successful leaders in any walk of life have invested hours in building a shared understanding.

Before London was successful in being chosen to host the 2012 Olympics, Tony Blair and Seb Coe spent many hours talking individually with all those who had a key vote. The vision of the Olympics in London was useless without a shared understanding that the city was geared up to deliver the Olympic vision in 2012. Buying-in to that vision was not only the result of lots of analysis and hard work, it was – crucially – the building of partnerships with those who mattered. Delivering the Olympics themselves will depend on a myriad of partnerships to make it work.

Sandy Millar was for twenty years the Vicar of Holy Trinity, Brompton in London. His church had a vision for encouraging Christian learning across a very wide spectrum. The Alpha Course has been a great success in both the UK and internationally. At the heart of this success was a willingness to build partnerships with a wide range of churches of different denominations and traditions. It was a combination of clarity of thought and a personal warmth that was insightful and inspirational, which helped to build buy-in to this radical vision – of Alpha courses where people from hugely diverse backgrounds could grow in their understanding of faith. The Bishop of Kensington wrote of Sandy Millar, 'He is a priest who has always shown great generosity with both his vision and his time. His visionary and sensitive leadership and his generosity of spirit have been instrumental in people, plant and money being renewed.'

It is worth reflecting on these questions:

- How good am I at building partnerships?
- Are there particular partnerships that I could be developing?
- What shared vision can help strengthen these partnerships?

Recognise opportunities and respond to them

A clear vision must be grounded in current reality and be flexible enough to take account of the needs of your partner and dependents. It also needs to be able to take account of opportunities and respond to them. Whatever your game plan for the future, there will always be unpredictable events. Some jobs will close down and others will open up. Decisions will affect members of your family which knock into your other priorities. The needs in different organisations will change and opportunities will suddenly occur where adaptability is paramount.

This does not mean scanning the appointments page in every newspaper every week, but it does mean keeping an eye on changes that might affect you. Occasionally it can be useful to use the following discipline and reflect on:

- What sort of opportunities might I be interested in?
- How much effort is it worth putting into keeping a careful eye on what wider opportunities there might be?
- How will I test whether the opportunities that arise have any merit?
- What range of different sorts of spheres might my skills be applied in?
- What other opportunities would give me particular joy?
- Have I reached the stage where a drop in income would be fine in order to take forward opportunities that are particularly attractive to me?

Michael had set his heart on doing a particular sort of job at board level and was very focused on this aspiration. Perhaps he was too focused, because when it came to interview he tended to be tense and not give of his best. A new option came up as chief executive in a different organisation. Various people encouraged him to apply and he did so in a rather half-hearted way. He prepared carefully for the interview but was not worried about it. Because he was less tense and more relaxed he did a superb interview and was offered the job. Initially he hesitated about accepting it. When the Chair of the organisation began to look elsewhere he began to appreciate how attractive this option was, grasped it wholeheartedly and is very focused on making a success of it.

There was a danger that Michael's vision was so focused on a conventional pathway of success that he did not recognise this alternative opportunity. It had the advantage that he was more relaxed as he went through the process and clearly did well. He needed friends around him who kept talking about this option and encouraged him to recognise it as a wonderful opportunity. There was a danger that he was too loyal to the organisation he was currently in and didn't recognise as strongly as he should have done that now was the time to move on.

Create your own success

There is a delicate balance between the strength to visualise success and the humility to recognise your limitations. It is not either/or. Delivering personal vision depends on the confidence to believe that success is possible. A group of high-potential civil servants from ethnic minorities on the Pathways programme (run jointly by the Cabinet Office and Praesta Partners) recently did some research called 'A Framework for Success' looking at how best individuals could progress to senior positions. Their conclusions focused on three key words:

- **Being:** what makes a candidate credible for a senior post.
- **Looking:** where do the opportunities lie and how do I get to them?
- **Doing:** what is required and the process of preparation.

Their advice under **being** was:

- build a reputation through a good record of delivery,
- be visible, e.g. work on high-profile jobs,
- focus on good interpersonal skills,
- make others aware of your achievements, and
- build your own confidence and self-belief.

Under **looking**:

- identify opportunities,
- use mentors and senior sponsors,
- draw upon networks, and
- position yourself to attract opportunities.

Under **doing**:

- apply for jobs – raise your profile and gain experience, widen your network,
- market yourself – make contact with potential employers, get yourself to the interview stage,
- do your research – demonstrate you have thought about the job and what you would do, and
- prepare thoroughly – conduct a dry interview run.

Their concluding illustration was the 'oomph' factor necessary to win the Olympic bid. The Paris bid was technically almost perfect and completely followed the IOC rules. The London bid was characterised by creativity, embracing wider implications, innovation, hard work and a strong belief that it could be successful. This oomph factor came from a combination of self-belief, trying new things and hard work. The people involved in the London bid were echoing the advice from Benjamin Franklin: 'By failing to prepare, you are preparing to fail.'

Build your reputation

Delivering your own personal vision depends partially on that vision being recognised by others. Rachel, a senior manager from an ethnic minority background, talks of the importance of establishing a strong reputation. She puts a great store on first impressions. She has trained herself to be good at giving a positive first impression. This is based on spending a moment collecting herself before important conversations and then being overtly present in each conversation. It is about never losing heart because you never know what the outcome will be from each discussion. Once a positive initial rapport has been established, it provides a basis for a reputation to be built based on both personal impact, clarity and warmth. From that basis a reputation flows and is generated by word of mouth.

Once a reputation is established then it is far easier to work towards a shared vision. As rapport is built up, sharing elements of a personal vision in conversation can build up an empathy which leads to allies and then fellow travellers towards the same vision.

Visioning that goes round corners

Sometimes individuals have a clear vision of who they want to be. The girl at 15 who is clear that she wants to train to be doctor has a clarity of motivation that can carry her through a working life in medical practice. That single-mindedness is wonderful to behold but rare. Lifelong visions *are* rare; often we move three steps forward and two steps back. It would be nice to be able to see round corners but often our line of vision changes when we reach one. We are constantly having to adapt and shift. An iterative approach is often necessary to ensure a freshness about our dreams.

If we have too fixed a vision we can become arrogant in trying to ensure we deliver it and over-anxious if things begin to go wrong. Tunnel vision is the worst sort of vision because you are blind to the changing environment. If we force ourselves to keep listening, observing and communicating, our vision will be open to change and evolve.

One way to look at this is to see our vision as a journey with base camps along the way. As we reach key base camps it gives us time to reflect on whether we are still destined for the peak of the Himalayas. Once we have concluded that this is indeed our destination we can go single-mindedly to the next base camp and then review again. Aiming for base camps reduces that uncertainty and forces us to take stock at key moments.

Judith, until recently a Senior Manager in a UK financial institution, is now taking a career break and re-evaluating her next steps. She says that she never had a strong vision and envied people who did; she was ambitious but not always certain what drove her. She had fulfilled her expectations more than she had expected. There was a lot of gut feel and intuitive logic. She had been trying to prove something to herself: her vision was about progressing, learning and financial reward.

Now her thinking about her vision is wider. She is not wanting just a vision about financial reward and is thinking hard about what she wants to do for the rest of her life. It is scary. It is a journey she wants to embark on in order to find a vision that she is entirely at home with. For too long she felt that she had been driven by the expectations of her family, herself and the institutions she worked for. She is not critical of her employer at all: it is just that she needs to go on her own journey to become clear about her vision. She is confident that after a few months on a career break she will be back in a senior management role in another organisation. She certainly has huge skills of determination with a strong track record of success. What she will come back with after her break is a much stronger coherence in her personal vision: she will be more strategic and therefore more effective in her job.

I met Judith three months after the start of her career break; she looked so well and had done a lot of travelling and thinking. There was a freshness about her approach, her personal vision was beginning to reshape. She didn't want to rush that transformation. She would begin to look for specific jobs in a month's time. What matters to her most in her next job is going to be very different; she will do her work with great energy and skill but will see it in a wider context of what is most important for her in personal terms.

Keep your vision fluid

Peter Senge and his colleagues talk about keeping the vision fluid. They advise against using the words 'etched in stone'. Their perspective is that 'visions are always evolving: they are an expression of our heart's desire. As we work towards our vision, we learn more about ourselves and other possibilities become clearer'.

The following two examples illustrate the value of allowing a personal vision to be fluid. A friend, Anna, talked about how she was losing faith in herself. She was worrying about things that she had no control over, and she was trying to do everything. Because she was so focused on an end goal which was becoming less and less attainable, she was sinking into apathy. She had the opportunity of a new job and hesitated about moving into this very different role. Her vision of herself had become vague and diluted. Her confidence had been dashed by the attitude of a couple of bosses who could not bring out the best in her.

Eventually she decided to accept the new job. She started the first day apprehensively: after a couple of weeks and some words of praise from her new boss it was as if a burden had been lifted from her shoulders. Her faith in herself was reborn and there was a new confidence. She even walked in a more positive and upright way.

Anna was so relieved that she had allowed herself to believe that her vision of herself was not irrevocably squashed. Her vision was re-ignited in a way that was ever stronger. One year on Anna is doing the new job successfully and has built her confidence to the point that it is unlikely to be completely squashed again.

Hazel had been determined to do her job well: she had worked at the same school for many years and had made a great impact on a generation of difficult children. She reflected that maybe she should have tried to move on earlier as she had become very typecast after twenty-two years in the same school.

She felt that perhaps she had become too focused on the immediate goal and not on the journey. If there had been a fluidity about her personal vision maybe she would have moved on sooner. Her wonderful doggedness in focusing on each generation of children was both a strength and a drawback. She decided to stay put because the pleasure she got from teaching was probably going to be greater than any pleasure she might gain from holding a senior post.

It might be worth reflecting on:

- How fluid is your personal vision?
- What are the fixed points you do not want to change?
- Is it helpful to see yourself on a journey with a vision that is evolving?
- How has that vision changed over the last year and how do you want it to change over the forthcoming year?

Ground your vision in current personal reality

There is no point in having a vision for ourselves that is completely unrealistic. If you live with your family in an isolated village in the north of England and there is no realistic prospect that they would willingly move the 250 miles south to London, then moving to London as a family is not an option. We can sometimes delude ourselves that changing the perspective of key individuals is going to happen. Sometimes it will, but if the process of trying to change perspective has been lengthy with no change in a shared view then it is time to accept the inevitable. Our vision does need to depend on the perspective of those closest to us. We cannot pretend that attitudes change easily. If we do we will eat away at ourselves and gradually lose some of our own self-belief. A frank discussion with your partner might cover the following:

- How similar are our priorities?
- What is the compatibility between the time commitment we want to give to work and career development?
- How can we provide enough space for each other to develop interests which fit into our wider vision of fulfilment?
- Are we balancing effectively the priority we give to our dependents as against fulfilling our own individual aspirations?

In a world where both parents are often employed, many oscillate between wanting to progress in their own jobs and being guilty about not being there for their children. There is no right or wrong answer about one or both parents working. It is crucial that parents work through to a conclusion which they can live with. The vision for one parent may be full-time employment and for the other part-time employment: it might be for the roles to switch round at a later date.

The needs of children are infinitely unpredictable. A vision that is too rigid can risk damaging family life. Flexibility to take account of children's needs has to be there if the family is to survive.

Accept life-changing moments that shape the vision

Holding on to a vision that is flexible is necessary both because of changes in the employment market and the wider world but also because of changes in personal circumstances.

Such changes could be something like:

- the death of a parent,
- the illness of a spouse,
- physical injury or depression in your children,
- a health risk that affects you personally,
- a shift in the international or domestic economy which directly affects your business, or
- a change in the government which means radically different priorities.

Some of these changes will generate anger or anxiety. When it is anger, living through it and coming out on the other side is not easy, but the anger will subside. When it causes anxiety, keep talking to your friends and do not be too surprised if they feed back to you some of the positive aspects of your situation. These life-changing moments may make you reflect on whether your personal vision is right. Reshaping your vision at critical points is not failure, it is using your freedom of choice and flexibility in a responsive and responsible way.

Some life-changing moments are painful but others can be very positive, such as:

- the arrival of a new child,
- the offer of early retirement,
- the growth of your children into fully fledged adults, or
- the celebration of a significant birthday.

These life-changing moments can be seen as a valuable part of the overall vision and not as completely separate from it. Most of us are bad at celebrating life-changing moments. If we promised ourselves that we would celebrate successes there would be a richness about our vision: life would be less of a long wait of expectation.

Stephen had just been appointed to a new job. He was going to spend the week-end before preparing and had told his family that he would be working for part of each weekend for the forthcoming months. A friend encouraged him to celebrate the new job by going out for a meal with his family and then marking the end of the first and second months with a family night out. Reluctantly he agreed – much to the delight of his family. It made a huge difference to his family's attitude to the new job.

Develop a personal impact that is consistent with your self-image

Sometimes there is a surprising discontinuity between our self-image and the impact we have on people. We want to be regarded as forward-thinking, but we spend a lot of time bogged down in the detail. We want to be generous with our time and energy and yet we fill every moment of the day. We want to be decisive and yet we procrastinate.

We will never get a perfect match between our self-image and our impact on others. But striving to get that right is important to ensure consistency. If our colleagues see us as aspiring to one vision and doing the opposite they will be wary about getting close to us. Linked with trying to ensure this coherence is a willingness to admit when our personal impact and our vision of ourselves are not in line. This sense of confession is not a sign of weakness but of great strength.

Jean is managing director of a regional organisation. She says that her vision used to be about achieving a certain level of seniority within the organisation: once there, her vision became more about how she was going to make a difference within the organisation and how she could add value. Now that she is well established at this senior level she says that her vision is to improve her emotional intelligence so that she can be more intuitive in a range of situations so that she attunes quickly to where people are coming from.

Her vision is to increase her sensitivity in being able to weigh people and situations up quickly. The aspiration has moved on from what she should do to how best she can do it. She wants to be able to make a positive difference as effectively as possible. She says that the promotion to MD has brought pressures, but it has been the making of her in terms of focusing her ambition away from just attaining seniority to making a personal impact through understanding people and situations more quickly.

Watch the negative vision

A positive vision can have a positive effect but it can have a negative consequence too. If we build a vision up too much we can be destined for disappointment. If the top job is all that will satisfy us, then the probability is that we will not be successful.

Can we be both focused and resilient enough to cope with inevitable reverses? Part of the balance may be a clear vision about next steps coupled with an acceptance that not reaching that vision still means more progress than might otherwise have happened. Your aspiration as a teacher might be for all your pupils to reach a certain grade, but if three are unsuccessful that does not mean you have failed as a teacher. Without the clarity of your efforts maybe many more would have been unsuccessful. Telling yourself that what looked like failure was success is never easy: often it is friends and colleagues who can be more objective than you in seeing the real progress that has been made.

There are often moments of self-doubt when our minds fill with gloomy visions. How do we cope with the seeds of doubt behind the fear or the persistent fears which undermine the vision so that it begins to disappear? Self-doubt can be healthy in bringing a sense of realism, but it can also be very damaging if it erodes our self-worth. There is nothing more sad then seeing a talented individual so wracked by fears that they take no risks and either avoid all employment or deliberately fill a role which does not use their skills effectively.

How can you best cope with self-doubt?

- Keep a strong focus on your values.
- Enable others to encourage and challenge you.
- Keep in mind what has worked well in the past.
- Ensure that some of your aspirations for the future are deliverable.

Be accurate about your self-vision before an interview

Going for an interview is such an instructive way of clarifying your vision. It is about:

- a vision about what is needed in the particular job,
- a vision of how you would deliver in that job, and
- an understanding of how you are likely to be perceived by others at interview.

As I prepare people for interview I press them about their clarity and coherence in the way they express their vision. I also have a clear perspective on the personal impact they have on me as interviewer: I work with them on what perspective they want the interviewer to have. What do they think is the interviewer's mental picture of their commitment, their contribution and their passion? It is not only a matter of having a vision. It is, crucially, how it is communicated and whether it can persuade others.

Avoid complacency

A successful athlete is continually stretching the boundaries: the world record for the 100 metres keeps getting broken. A personal vision that is demanding provides a clear focus. There are times when we need to relax our personal goals because the initial ones have proved to be unrealistic, but there is also a time to stretch your goals. Organisations are continually setting more demanding targets, whether it is delivering examination results, reducing waiting lists or meeting financial targets. These targets have got to be passed on to those working within the organisation. Continually stretching goals in a way which engenders rather than dampens energy requires careful judgement both in how we manage ourselves and those who work for us. The need for ever more demanding targets will not go away. Getting the balance right in terms of the 'carrot and stick' incentives both for ourselves and others is one of the most demanding tasks of leadership.

If we know that the required outcomes of the vision for which we are responsible are to become tighter how best can we approach it? It could be:

- Drawing from our previous experience where we have made significant progress.
- Putting milestones on the way that are realistic.
- Ensuring effective rewards and acknowledgement both for ourselves and our colleagues.

Celebrate

Celebrate at every available opportunity. When we set up Praesta Partners as an independent organisation specialising in executive coaching we celebrated with buns on the first day, champagne on day two, a launch for 400 guests in month three, a reception for all the suppliers and contractors who had helped get us up and running in month four and an awayday in Bruges in month five. We kept marking reaching key milestones. It did not make us complacent, it made us more energised for the future.

Both as an individual and part of a corporate organisation, how can you celebrate success more? It might be through cakes, an evening drink, a warm message of thanks or an outing. The best way of ensuring a vision happens is deliberately to keep celebrating every step of the way. Create the stories of good times as an individual or as a team which can keep you going when times are tougher.

A long-term vision is not a requirement

You may not have a strong personal vision. That may be absolutely right and nothing to feel uneasy about. For example, you might be:

- enjoying your job so much that you do not particularly want to focus on the future,
- preoccupied with raising children or looking after elderly relatives (you know that in the future there will be the opportunity to re-evaluate your next steps),
- recognising that future uncertainties are so great that there is no point planning ahead, or
- living for the present and knowing that you are not doing any damage for the future.

You might consciously be saying to yourself:

- I will define more of a vision but not yet.
- I want the vision for my life to be consistent with my partner's next steps.
- Other responsibilities rightly mean that my own personal vision must be put on hold.

Your focus might be on the next job and not on a long-term vision.

Andrew Higginson, the Finance and Strategy Director at Tesco, says that he has never focused on a personal vision. He did not have a life plan. He had never envisaged earlier in his life that he would become a board member of Tesco. His approach was always to look for the next most fulfilling job. He was continually wanting to expand his horizons and grow through doing new challenges. Advancement was a driver, but never with a specific long-term vision.

Andrew's vision was about doing the next job effectively, not about a long-term aspiration. That approach clearly worked well for him. It is worth reflecting on what sort of vision is most helpful for you: is it long term or short term? It could equally well be about your long-term aspiration or how you will do the next job. Either is valid: the key test is that you are honest with yourself in defining what type of future vision is going to be most helpful to you.

Stretch your thinking

Suma Chakrabarti was born in India and came to England as a boy. He has had an outstanding career within the Civil Service reaching the level of Permanent Secretary at the Department for International Development. At each stage in his career a sense of vision has been important to him. When he became Permanent Secretary at the Department for International Development he began the job with a vision about management reform. Shortly after he arrived he published a vision document called 'Strength to Strength'. For him, a strong sense of vision is crucial in order to provide a context for people working in the organisation. Suma's view from his personal experience is that when he has a clear personal vision he is energised and is able to make his biggest impact. His advice is

> 'Do not be imprisoned by your in-tray. Look up. Think through how you are going to change things for the better. After you have been in a job for a few weeks think through what your personal vision is in making a difference. Try to draw threads together from your experience so far. You can always improve your organisation. But do link your vision to concrete changes you can be a part of helping to deliver. Be courageous.'

The danger with the word vision is that it can be over-used and ambiguous. It can, though, be a powerful term as a means of us focusing on who we want to be and what the impact is that we want to have on others. Some concluding questions:

- Do you have a clear vision for your future?
- What are the key ingredients of that vision covering your work, family and wider community?
- Is that vision consistent with your intellectual, physical, emotional and spiritual concerns?
- Is your vision flexible and adaptable?
- Are there clear milestones along the way?
- Do you take enough opportunities to reflect on whether your vision is

coherent across different aspects of your life and whether it is flexible enough to take account of changing circumstances?

- Is your vision realistic and challenging?
- Are you at one with those you love about the vision you are aspiring to?
- In that vision, what are the relative priorities of work, family, community and personal fulfilment? Are you content that they are in a proper balance?

Chapter 3:

Values

Nothing is more unpleasant than a virtuous person with a mean mind.

Walter Bagehot

Many of us were brought up with the assumption that it is bad manners to ask somebody about their politics or religion. We have moved on from that inhibition, but there is still the same reluctance to ask somebody about what values are most important to them. But we talk increasingly about what values an organisation is trying to espouse. We look out carefully for the wording that an organisation uses to describe its values while sometimes being reluctant to articulate our own. I encourage you not to be shy in being clear about the values that are most important to you, how they are changing, how you want them to change and how they will help you benchmark your own success. My hope is that you will want to keep refreshing your values through a range of life experiences.

Understanding our own values and how they drive us is crucial to:

- understanding why we react in particular ways,
- understanding our motivations in different situations,
- clarifying how we interlink our personal and work priorities,
- enabling us to make the best possible contribution in chosen work or community activities, and
- seeing where the synergy best lies between our personal contribution and the preferences of groups or organisations of which we are a part.

Key themes in this chapter are about:

- Where your values come from,
- What values drive you,
- The interplay between personal and organisational values,
- Illustrations of particular values and their impact,
- Clarifying your values.

Where do your values come from?

In this chapter the definition of values I am using is 'beliefs or behaviours that are of particular importance to an individual in the way they live their life and interact with other people'. This covers the way individuals interact with people within their families, communities and at work. It is about individual values with a recognition of the important interplay between personal and corporate values.

Personal values often result from:

- Beliefs about the right or wrong way of doing things which may or may not have a religious basis.
- Moral judgements which may be based on a view about what is right and wrong in absolute terms, or be based on relative assessments about the most appropriate action in particular situations.
- Intellectual assumptions about an approach or behaviour that will produce acceptable results.
- Experience which either explicitly or implicitly tells us that a particular form of behaviour will produce the best sort of results.

Personal values often relate to:

- The outcomes that we think are important in our jobs or family and community life.
- The standards we set.
- The nature of how we interrelate with other people in our inner circle, be it in the family, the community or work situation.
- The way we interrelate with the wider circle of people we meet, be they work colleagues, neighbours or customers.
- The way we use our time and resources.

Organisational values tend to follow a similar pattern. They are about:

- The outcomes that are most important to the organisation.
- The standards and behaviours expected in the way work is carried out.
- The way people within the organisation work with and respect each other.
- Standards in relation to dealing with external people such as stakeholders, shareholders, customers or the media.
- The way resources are used within the organisation, be they time, experience or financial resources.

Our values come from a mixture of sources. At a personal level they can come from our family, our culture, our religion, our practical experience and our intellectual beliefs. Sometimes one aspect of our background will create in us a very powerful driver for good in terms of a powerful value which resonates with the needs in a particular situation. At other times a value that drives us hard can make us blinkered to the realities of a particular situation and mean we become ineffectual. Hence the importance of us being objective about our values, where they come from, what they are, how they drive us and whether we want to be driven in a particular way.

We are making compromises every day in the use of our time and energy. One of our values might be the importance of providing a strong source of encouragement for our colleagues. We are always having to interrelate that value to our time commitments and to judgements about the quality of the work being done. Demonstrating encouragement is something we might be assessing ourselves on regularly, being clear that the encouragement is not being done in a vacuum unconnected with current realities. It is perfectly possible to have a belief that it is important to provide encouragement for particular colleagues every week, but how it is done will vary depending on the situation and their likely response. Platitudinous encouragement for its own sake can be futile. Encouragement that is rooted in particular situations with practical words looking to the future can be both relevant and influential.

What personal values drive you?

Personal values have a powerful influence on the way we operate in our work. A couple of examples illustrate the range of influence of personal values.

Michael moved rapidly through different jobs within the public sector to reach the post of chief executive of a national organisation. He is clear that an important value to him is the importance of public service. He in no way undervalues the contribution of those in the private sector; for him personally he is clear that he would not enjoy as his work 'making widgets or money'. He has thoroughly enjoyed the opportunities he has had to take forward government policy in sensitive and important areas. This has brought huge intellectual and personal satisfaction. He readily admits, though, that one of his great pleasures outside work is making intricate engineering models even though a career in the manufacturing sector has never held any attraction.

For Michael a crucial part of his values has come from the stability of family life. He was the middle one of five siblings and has always got on very well with his family. A stable marriage and friendships have also been very important to him. There have been sadnesses but the strength of his home life and family bonds have been fundamental to him. It is that quality of interaction within his home life that he wants to replicate in his dealings with others and in the culture of the organisations where he has had a leading role. One of Michael's strengths is that he is willing to be very open about the values that are important to him and how he wants to grow and change in the light of those values.

Sadeka held a team leader position in a national financial organisation. An overriding personal value for her was the importance of giving and receiving love. She had been in a job which had been a very painful experience, she had worked very hard but not been appreciated by her boss. Her joy had gradually gone, she had been striving for perfection and not reaching it. She became increasingly depressed and needed a break from work.

Her best therapist was her daughter, whose constant cheerfulness and encouragement had meant that she regained her equanimity. She is now back at work in a new role feeling loved by her family and supported by her colleagues. She now sees 'perfection' as an ugly word: by focusing on perfection she had set herself up to fail. Out of adversity the value of striving for perfection had been replaced by the value of allowing herself to be loved by her family and then building mutual support with those in the workplace. The result was a much happier person and a more effective manager.

These two illustrations reflect the importance of personal values. For Michael it is strengths of his home life and family bonds, and for Sadeka it is the importance of giving and receiving love. Both have been successful in their own spheres based on acknowledging the importance of their personal values.

Do we:

- Fully recognise the personal values that are important to us?
- Allow ourselves to embrace those values rather than dismiss them?
- Acknowledge those values to others?

How captive are we to our inherited values?

For most people the most powerful values impacting upon them come from their family or religious roots. The following are four examples where inherited values have been very important but which have also changed over time.

George is the chief executive of a major engineering manufacturing concern. He grew up in a working class family in Scotland. He was competitive with a fiery temper. Even at primary school he was always a driver; recognition and reward were always important. When he was aged 11 he did a milk round with the income all going straight to his mother (except the tips, which he kept!). He played schoolboy football at international level. He was always willing to take on responsibility. When he left school he took on an apprenticeship in a steel works.

He inherited his mother's work ethic. He wanted to better himself and was always looking for new opportunities. As he moved up he did not have a vision that was a long way forward, but he did have a lot of self-belief and always focused on the best he could do. He moved from being quality director in one organisation to quality director in another, eventually becoming managing director and was then recruited through open competition for a major CEO post.

The drive and commitment that came from his mother and his working-class background is still very evident. He describes his key values as honesty, integrity, logic and reason. Delivering promises is important. Consistency is an essential part of his own self-belief. He says

> 'The key issue is the ability to take decisions that other people often think are right but have not managed to be able to decide. There is an important need to drive things through. I had to make 500 people redundant. I could look everybody in the eye and say it was the right thing to do for the business to survive. If I had not done so the business would have collapsed. Objectivity and clarity of thinking is crucial.'

George fully recognises that competitiveness is important to him. 'Engulf your competition with yourself, not others. I am externally driven. I believe the importance of doing a good job. I let others get on with it but where necessary I can wield a long screwdriver!'

His single-mindedness draws heavily on his personal values of honesty, integrity, logic and reason. There is an utter objectivity in his approach which has enabled him to create successful outcomes in successive jobs. He has shown a determination to maintain as many good quality jobs for staff as possible amidst changing economic and political circumstances. He has had to cope with criticism and his value set has been an important part of retaining his sanity.

Gloria was brought up in Guyana where her parents were both successful lawyers. Education was strongly part of her culture and background, and when her parents came to the UK they maintained this focus on education. She trained as a lawyer and now holds a very senior position in the legal profession. She exudes a warm, positive approach and yet she is always challenging. She works in a part of the country where the leadership tends to be white, male and aged over 50. Gloria is female, young and black. She has not let being different daunt her: recently she was an outstanding speaker at a school speech day. She has rebuilt positive relationships with key leaders in the region. Her outgoing positive approach based on valuing learning, reinforcing the positive and facing people up to the need for change has had such a powerful effect. Gloria is a superb example of someone having a clarity of values which is then lived out. Her background, different from others in the region, has proved to be an enabler in terms of her having a crucial impact.

Jean, MD of a regional organisation, has been leading major change in a very difficult environment. She comes from an ethnic minority background and has worked very hard to make a successful career. She is generous in acknowledging those who have contributed to her success by enabling her to have the opportunities to do well. A key value for her is always respecting your colleagues and never being critical or disrespectful of others. Her values have not changed in terms of the importance of respect for colleagues. What has changed as she has moved into senior roles is a greater awareness of the contribution of others. She says that the shift is between values that drive you as an individual and enabling others to be able to contribute effectively.

Salem is one of the most conscientious managers I have ever met. The strongest value for him is service, which he describes as coming from his mother's strong Sikh faith. For his mother, serving others was what gave her greatest joy: this was passed on so clearly to her son. As a specialist within a big organisation he is consulted by innumerable people for his advice. He is always willing to serve them. This is his greatest strength but also, he fully acknowledges, his biggest work issue. He recognises that he needs to prioritise more and more. Serving others is so much a driver that saying 'Sorry, I can't help you at this point because I've got to deliver a report,' doesn't come easily to him.

These value drivers, whether it is the Protestant work ethic or the Sikh focus on service, are important but need to be seen in a wider context. If we are too utterly focused on one dimension of value we can destroy others and ourselves. Salem is beginning to rebalance his time commitments so that he is fulfilling his value of serving others in helping to deliver long-term changes as well as meeting short-term requests. These four examples illustrate the strength of inherited values, the importance of building on them and sometimes moving on from them.

It is worth reflecting on:

- What inherited values are most evident in the way we live our lives?
- Have we fully embraced the strength of these inherited values?
- How have these inherited values changed?
- How do we want them to evolve further?

What professional values drive you?

In different spheres there are explicit or implicit values associated with particular types of work. Sometimes there is a very strong professional code of ethics, sometimes it is more custom and practice that drive the values. What follows are some examples from individuals where professional values have been very important drivers. As you read them it is worth reflecting on whether there are particular professional values that are driving you.

John Dunford, as General Secretary of the Association of School and College Leaders, describes his values in his current role as rooted in his years as a school teacher. For him keeping up his professionalism is important: you have 'street cred' because of your background in the profession. It is important to keep the sensitivity of what it is like to be in other people's shoes. The main value that drove him was bringing opportunities to ordinary kids both when he was a head teacher and in his current role. They were the same values in both his roles: as head of a school or in his national work. As a school head, he wanted to create the environment in which school leaders could do their job effectively: it was enabling individuals to develop their expectations about what they could achieve. He set great store when he was a head teacher of creating a climate in which both teachers and pupils recognised they had talents in a whole range of different areas and developed the courage to use those talents to the best of their ability.

For Jenny, working at a senior level in a national financial institution, the key values were fairness and honesty. Fairness was crucial in the way the organisation operated and in the way people interrelated with each other. There were bound to be moments of compromise: 10 per cent compromise was OK but a 50 per cent compromise in terms of fairness made her feel uncomfortable. What made her most concerned was when power was used in a selfish way which resulted in unfairness. Pragmatism is necessary, but unless there is a strong spirit of fairness in the way people are dealt with then the success of the organisation is undermined. Jenny's linked theme was honesty. Facts could always be presented in a variety of different ways, but when someone was economical with the truth suspicion and distrust were the potential results. Any organisation must be seen to be basically honest or there will be a point when people within the organisation begin to think it is not being straight with them about the realities of the future.

When Richard became the chief executive of an international organisation he thought hard about the values he felt strongly about. Values had been a very important explicit guideline for him in his two previous roles. He described the values that for him stood the test of time as:

- Integrity: being open and honest.
- People: valuing and developing people.
- Customers: adding value in helping customers achieve their objectives.
- Teamwork: working with shareholders to achieve objectives.
- Innovation: challenge and invention.

These are important measures of self-assessment in his new CEO role. His strong belief is that integrity is the most important of the values: if you are not regarded as open and honest your credibility as chief executive is much undermined. This can be vital in an international environment where there are various cultures. Some of the aspects of living his values include the following:

- Integrity: not having secret agendas and being vigorous in working through the key issues with his staff.

- People: being very explicit in appreciating the contribution of all the individuals he meets from the receptionist to board members.
- Customers: getting to know the customers well and understanding their perspective.
- Teamwork: building teams within the organisation in an explicit and positive way, and building a spirit of partnership with key stakeholders developing shared agendas.
- Innovation: always setting a tone of ensured ideas are challenged and developed with new perspectives being welcomed.

For John, this is a professional value of enabling individuals to develop their expectations about what they can achieve. For Jenny, it is the importance of fairness and honesty, and for Richard it is integrity. All are determined to live their professional values to the full.

Are we:

- Clear about the professional values that relate to us?
- Consistent in the way we apply them?
- Respectful of other people's professional values?

How do our values cope with major external change?

We can sometimes be self-righteous about our values. Of course this belief is right, we assert. Sometimes honest self-reflection about how our values have changed or not changed is important. Sometimes our values change imperceptibly over a period because we are influenced by different individuals or situations. On other occasions a life-changing event can quite dramatically affect our values. A key step is to be absolutely honest in looking at how change affects us and how we respond to that change. The following two examples are of senior leaders who have reflected hard on whether their values have changed.

David Adleman is principal of a successful sixth form college. He is clear that his own values have been derived from his own background. Both his parents came from working-class backgrounds and education was, for them, the passport to ideas and culture and to a higher standard of living than their own parents had been able to provide. But education was not merely a means of achieving social advancement; it was also an end in itself – both parents became teachers and his father went on to be a university lecturer. On his father's side of the family there was also a strong Jewish tradition of valuing learning for its own sake. And his mother, coming from a Barnsley mining background, was imbued with the traditions of working-class self-help and betterment through knowledge. It is no surprise then that David has a passionate commitment to the power of education as a force for good in society.

For him, leading an educational institution is based on the central value of a love of learning. He is fully committed to promoting education in its own right because of the personal value he holds about the importance of education. At the same time he is fully committed to ensuring the highest possible qualifications to provide opportunities for the youngsters whatever his personal views on whether the government should be changing the examination arrangements for 18-year-olds. One of the dimensions where his personal values impact strongly on his leadership is his belief that within learning for young people there should be opportunities for enrichment in artistic, aesthetic and spiritual areas.

David readily admits that his background has given him a passion to do the best possible job he can as a college principal. He recognises that there have been defining moments when he has adapted his approach and ambition. He is honest in describing the balance between his core values and pragmatism. That has not undermined his values, it has just made them more shaped and consistent. To his college governors and staff he is focused on the success of the college and its students while having a very strong sense of care for all those engaged in this educational endeavour.

Ken Boston has held very senior leadership roles in Australia and the UK. As Chief Executive of the UK Qualifications and Curriculum Council he has faced many leadership dilemmas. For him values are about ethics, morality and fair play. These fundamentals have to be followed, modelled and displayed: as a leader you must be seen as a person of integrity and credibility, and be scrupulous in personal relations. Ken is clear that his values at their core have not changed. It is about honesty, integrity and doing your best to achieve excellence. He readily admits that he is driven to work hard by the Protestant work ethic.

In professional terms, as an educational leader, he has focused on the value of equity of opportunity and outcomes. A just society is a strong motivator. As a public servant he believes it important to make speeches that are formative in terms of promoting fairness and equality. The organisation he now leads is focused on quality and standards; therefore, he must be consistent with that in his own leadership. He sees it as important to be focusing on thought leadership so that within the framework of government policy he is not afraid to explore the implications of that policy. Within the organisation itself he places a strong emphasis on fair dealing with people with the honest rewarding of virtue and providing positive assistance for those who are under-performing.

Both David and Ken have used their values as touchstones for their decisions. Both have a strong focus on core values which have been crucial in coping with change.

The relevance for us may be:

• Has external change helped shape our values?
• Are we content with the way we are balancing core values and pragmatism?
• Are our values robust enough to cope with major external change?

The interplay between individual and corporate values?

A very important area is the interplay between individual and corporate values, which is highly relevant for many of us. The interplay should be a two-way process. If values are going to have any impact in an organisation there must be an opportunity for people working in the organisation to influence the creation and living out of those values. If they are presented in a top-down way they will rapidly be ignored. If the consultation is vague and woolly with no clear and concise values result, then the whole process will be regarded as a waste of time. If the resulting values are wordy or fudged they will have no impact. The senior team need to define the final values in such a way that there is simplicity and clarity if they are going to have an impact, with individuals seeing consistency between personal and organisational values. They need to demonstrate that there has been a listening process going on, but at the end of the day it is their job to set clear and concise values. This section looks at a sequence of different examples.

Values will be at their most powerful when there is a synergy between personal and organisational values. After an extensive consultation period the Departmental Board of the Department of Education and Skills defined the following behaviours in 2002 as the centre point of the change it wanted to encourage:

- We are determined to make a difference.
- We listen and value diversity.
- We are honest and open.
- We innovate and challenge.
- We learn and improve.

The initial draft had been modified as a result of focus groups across the organisation, where the plea was for simplicity and clarity. Each of us who were members of the Departmental Board tried to build the behaviours into the organisation by living them as board members, constantly referring to them and then ensuring that living them was fully reflected in performance assessments. We recognised that the behaviours often needed to be linked together where an individual was deciding on a particular course of action. We recognised that there could well be a tension between 'we listen and value diversity' and 'we are determined to make a difference'. The challenge of living the behaviours was to reconcile these values in an open and frank way in order to reach the most appropriate conclusions.

The Board was very conscious that there needed to be a unity between personal and organisational values. As board members we needed to demonstrate these behaviours or the rest of the organisation would not take them seriously. We asked very openly to be challenged about whether the values were being lived. The fact that the behaviours were fully embedded meant that when there were major controversial issues there was a clear touchstone on which to base our reactions and assess how well we had done.

The behaviours which we adopted as the Board of the Department for Education and Skills worked because of the consultation, the clarity about the behaviours and the fact that we were continually testing whether we were living by them. I still carry that list of behaviours in my top pocket.

Although statements of values come in many different shapes and sizes there are often common themes. BNFL set up the British Nuclear Group in 2005 to focus on cleaning up the UK's nuclear legacy. Its values are to:

- Act with integrity and respect for others.
- Be safe and environmentally responsible.
- Commit to achieving success for our customers.

- Deliver value and profit.
- Excel in our operations.

British Nuclear Group describes itself as 'Customer driven, commercially focused and value for money'. It is in a clear commercial context that it states that 'Our values help to underpin the right attitudes, behaviours and relationships with stakeholders that are fundamental to good business.' The words of these values cover the areas identified at the start of the chapter:

- Outcomes: 'delivering value and profit'.
- Standards of work: 'be safe and environmentally responsible' and 'excelling in our operations'.
- Standards in relation to each other: 'act with integrity and respect for others'.
- Standards in relation to stakeholders and customers: 'commit to achieving success for our customers'.

A very different organisation, Mount Alvernia Hospital in Guildford, defines its health care values in the following way.

- Respect for each person: in our health care ministry we respect the dignity of each person, striving at all times to be courteous, understanding and compassionate.
- Holistic care: we are attentive to the needs of the people in our care, in the physical, psychological and spiritual aspects of their lives, helping them to attain healing, wholeness, harmony and inner peace.
- Hospitality: we endeavour to provide a warm, welcoming and peaceful atmosphere in all our hospitals and homes, and an environment which is conducive to holistic healing.
- Excellence in care: we strive diligently to provide quality care in all that we do. We encourage high standards of excellence and professionalism, supporting the ongoing professional and personal development of all our staff.
- Justice: we uphold the Christian principles of integrity and justice for those in our care, and in our relationships with our relatives, our staff and all with whom we do business.

There is a similarity between Mount Alvernia Hospital's values and those of the British Nuclear Group in that they both focus on:

- the excellence of what the organisation offers,

- personal standards of integrity and respect for others,
- the importance of the quality of relationships within the organisation, and
- the importance of working with customers effectively.

BNG has to be a highly commercial organisation with a strong focus on safety. Mount Alvernia Hospital is a Catholic independent hospital with a clear focus on health care. Both organisations need effective relationships with their customers, both have a strong focus on training, development and support, both place a strong emphasis on responsible stewardship through efficient management, sound financial administration and effective governance.

Accenture is a global management consulting, technology services and outsourcing company operating in a very commercial market. Accenture puts a lot of emphasis on skills, staff, style and shared values. Accenture is very clear that 'Our core values shape the culture and define the character of our company. They guide how we behave and make decisions'. Their core values are:

- Stewardship – Building a heritage for future generations, acting with an owner mentality, developing people everywhere we are, and meeting our commitments to all internal and external stakeholders.
- Best People – Attracting and developing the best talent for our business, stretching our people and developing a 'can do' attitude.
- Client Value Creation – Improving our clients' business performance, creating long-term, win-win relationships and focusing on execution excellence.
- One Global Network – Mobilising the power of teaming to deliver consistently exceptional service to our clients anywhere in the world.
- Respect for the Individual – Valuing diversity, ensuring an interesting and inclusive environment, and treating people as we would like to be treated ourselves.
- Integrity – Inspiring trust by taking responsibility, acting ethically, and encouraging honest and open debate.

In these Accenture core values there is a lot of focus on building trust, energy and excitement into the work. This is linked with a focus on innovation and wider care for the environment. For example, on every desk in the London office there is an upright cardboard container into which used or scrap paper is inserted; this is then collected and recycled. This is a powerful symbol about the value of recycling and respect for the environment. It also acts as a reminder to those working in Accenture about not wasting resources and time. It is a wonderful example of how focusing in a simple but clear way on one aspect can reinforce other values in a constructive way.

Diageo, an international food and beverage manufacturer, described a set of leadership capabilities in which living the values is central. These were:

- Ideas: an insatiable curiosity to identify new opportunities based on a clear understanding of how to grow and win in the marketplace.
- Living the values: demonstrates the behaviours that will build the strong business culture that supports our business ideas and goals.
- Emotional energy: the drive that leaders possess, actively communicate and demonstrate to create positive energy in others.
- Edge: the ability to face reality and take tough decisions about products, costs and people to deliver sustainable results.
- People performance: achieves growth by working through and with people, demonstrates the desire and ability to develop people.

These leadership capabilities demonstrate the importance of interlinking the difference aspects of any leadership prospectus. 'Living the values' is about behaviours which build a strong business culture. 'Ideas' is about vision. 'Edge' is a key ingredient in adding value. 'Emotional energy' and 'people performance' are all about focusing vitality.

Thinking positively about the link between the values of the organisation in which you work and your personal values is an essential step in focusing your contribution in a way that is effective within the organisation and that also gives personal satisfaction. Sometimes there will be such a discontinuity between our personal values and the organisation's values that you will want to move on. It is where there is reasonable synergy between our values and the organisation's values that we can make our most significant contribution. The issue is how we do this in a thoughtful and yet pragmatic way.

Reflecting on these examples:

- Are there aspects of the values for these organisations that surprise you?
- Are there themes from these values that might be relevant to you?

Developing and living a set of values

It is instructive to see how organisations have begun to put together key values and are taking them forward. In September 2005 the Home Office announced in a joint message from the then Permanent Secretary and the Home Secretary the following set of values.

Building a safe, just and tolerant society by:

- delivering for the public,
- being professional and innovative,
- working openly and collaboratively, and
- treating everyone with respect.

Some of the key points in a note to all staff when consulting about these values were:

- The overall objective of developing a set of values is to help the Home Office do its job of delivering our objectives and building a safer, just and tolerant society.
- Many organisations have gone down the road of creating a formal set of values which define their organisation's core of beliefs and principles. These values then guide the ways in which everyone in the organisation behaves towards each other and their external contacts and the sort of working practices that are used. We believe that having such a set of values will make the Home Office a better organisation to work with.
- We believe that it will also become a better place to work for our staff and that we will be a more effective organisation as a result.

The process they went through was as follows:

- The Group Executive Board heard presentations from two organis-ations which used values to drive their organisations and decided they wanted to take a values based approach, but only if there was sufficient support from staff.
- There was then wide consultation across the Home Office with the consensus being that it was worth developing Home Office values, but only if the values were more than just a good set of words and were also genuinely reflected in ways of working.
- A series of focus groups across the organisation and discussions with external stakeholders led to defining what might be the content of the values.

- There was a great deal of overlap between the views of the different groups about the importance of collaborative working, valuing people, professionalism and taking responsibility. Everyone wanted values that were short and memorable.
- Following the issuing of the proposed values there was staff consultation before settling the final wording.

The clear intention of David Normington, the new Permanent Secretary at the Home Office, is that these values are embedded with effective feedback about how they are working. The key challenge will be the way the values are used to make a tangible difference to the public, staff and stakeholders.

In Chapter 2, I looked at the vision that the Highways Agency has set out in 'Customers First'. They have linked the delivery of that vision very clearly to a set of values about how they are going to behave. These are:

- Customer service: we put our customers first.
- Teamwork: we work together in dynamic teams and partnerships.
- Improvement: we encourage learning, innovation and flexibility.
- Diversity: we value people for their diversity and contribution.
- Best value: we deliver effective services that provide value for money.
- Integrity: we build trust by acting with honesty and fairness.

The senior staff of the Highways Agency have linked together their vision and values through a clear 'Statement of Intent' signed by the thirty-six members of the senior management team which is posted visibly throughout the organisation. This Statement of Intent about living the values is:

- We bring 'Customers First' to life and are passionate about delivering it.
- We enthuse and empower people in the Agency to put customers first.
- We communicate clear customer service aims and objectives, understand how that affects our teams and listen to their feedback.
- We transform poor and ineffective performance into positive and effective delivery for our customers.
- We learn quickly from our mistakes and don't repeat them.
- We celebrate and share success.

Addleshaw Goddard is a UK partnership of lawyers which works with more than eighty FTSE 350 clients. It is the product of a merger that took place in 2003 and has a clear programme of expansion. It is heavily reliant on its people and has recently been through a process to articulate its values which reflect both the values of today and the aspirations for the future. They have worked hard to bring the values to life both for the benefit of the partnership as a whole and for those working within the partnership.

The consultation involved extensive use of workshops with individuals being asked to be explicit through a scoring system about existing standards. The aim was to encapsulate:

- What we are like when we are at our best.
- What does that look like and feel like?
- What would it take for us to be like this more often?

Individuals were strongly encouraged to bring their personal values into the discussions to ensure a strong empathy between personal and organisational values. The result was a definition of the 'AG Way' depicted as follows:

The AG Way

These five elements were the distillation of the consultation exercise and built strongly on the responses. Although the AG Way resulted from a consultation on values it is fascinating that all 4 Vs are embedded within it:

- 'business focused' is about vision,
- 'open and honest' is about values,
- 'dynamic' is about both values and vitality,
- 'determined to succeed' is about value-added, and
- 'team players' is about vitality.

A useful exercise is to reflect on how comfortable you would be with this type of list of values as personal values:

- Are you focused enough on providing practical and commercial solutions?
- Are you driven to find innovative solutions?
- Are you always fair and straightforward?
- Are you bringing out the best in everyone?
- Are you enjoying working together and respecting individuality?

The ideal is to be comfortable that the values cover the right areas while accepting that you may fulfil some of them better than others.

Looking at the values of different organisations and how they are taking them forward can be a very useful touchstone to reflect on how well your values match different situations. When you feel challenged by different values it is worth pausing to think why.

Keeping assessing the impact of values is as important organisationally as individually. A senior team for a national organisation recently looked at its organisation's published values in the terms of:

- How well known are the values?
- Are they fit for purpose for the future?
- How do we self-assess ourselves and the organisation on how well we are living the values?
- Which values are most important to us individually?
- What is success in taking forward the values?

This provided a useful framework for deciding on next steps in terms of how the senior team is going to work together in a strategic way in their leadership of the organisation. This is an example of how values can be an important touchstone for reflection about progress made and future steps for both senior teams and individuals.

Trust as a core value

Trust is a value which has always been important but which is now being given a higher profile. Sally Bibb and Jeremy Kourdi, in their book *Trust Matters*, have focused on the importance of trust as a key value for individuals and organisations. They regard it as a crucial ingredient of organisational health. They argue that trust gets people energised: it is essential to the sound health of an organisation. They challenge individuals and organisations to look at the importance of trust through the themes of the power of trust, the cost of lost trust, the destroyers of trust, how leaders build trust and building a culture of trust. According to the authors, leaders who focus on the value of building trust:

- have insight into themselves,
- create an atmosphere of expectation and trust, and take responsibility,
- have clear intent and are honest, without hidden agendas,
- have the organisation's and employees' best interests at heart,
- have credibility, are consistent and trust others,
- let others see their passion – it is obvious what they care about,
- speak from the heart, not just from the intellect,
- confront people without being confrontational,
- do not mind admitting they do not know, and
- have integrity and use power positively.

A key issue for every potential leader is how they build trust, keep it and use it positively. As soon as using trust positively begins to look like manipulation then trust can so rapidly be destroyed. The suspicion of being manipulated is perhaps the most damaging perspective that an individual can have on their boss. Trust means openness, as far as that is possible, in order for the trust to be seen to be genuine and not bordering into manipulation. Key tests for any leader are:

- Have I taken steps today to build up trust?
- When I have drawn upon someone's trust, have I then taken steps to renew it?
- Is there any sense in which individuals could feel manipulated by what I have said and done?
- How can I guard against that criticism of manipulation?

Chris Mellor was heavily involved in a major merger when AWG acquired Morrison Construction. This added 3,500 to the UK workforce of 6,000 who had had no exposure to the original vision and values introduced by AWG in 1997. Chris Mellor saw the challenge as being about building trust. He wrote 'There will be questions about two parts of the organisation and what each one means to the other. We have to create that trust and sense of purpose and direction and revisit the values and get a consensus'. His conclusion, quoted in *By the Skin of Our Teeth* edited by Clive Morton, was that 'the way we behaved, true to our values, has created a huge amount of goodwill'.

Andrew Higginson, in his role as Finance and Strategy Director for Tesco, sees trust and respect as the crucial values both for himself and the organisation of which he is part. His view is that 'Trust and respect go to the heart of large organisations. You have to trust people to do the right thing. You must not constrain staff too much by the rules. They are your most important asset'.

Andrew says that trust and respect are especially important to him as an individual. 'You need guiding principles that are applied consistently. I don't see myself as different to when I left school. Respecting people whatever their role has always been important to me.'

In terms of living your values, Andrew places a strong emphasis on the importance of consistency so that the values are reinforced. This is equally true for an individual as it is for an organisation.

Being committed to each other's success

Individual success is fulfilling, but even more powerful is when a group of people celebrate the success of a team where individuals have enabled other members of the team to give of their best.

The most successful boards I have been part of are when individuals have been overtly keen to celebrate each other's success. It is rare that this happens, but when it does it can have such a powerful motivating force for the good on the whole board. When I work with senior teams or boards a strong focus is on how they are going to recognise and celebrate each other's success. I recently worked with one senior team on:

- What were their key strategic priorities?
- How were they going to operate as a corporate unit and demonstrate to the rest of the organisation that they were united?
- What cross-cutting roles were each of them going to take on individually in order to pull together the threads of a quite disparate organisation?

- How would they measure their own success?
- What were the individual strengths that they each brought into the organisation?
- What were the areas on which they needed to develop their own contribution to the corporate good?

On the themes of strengths and areas of contribution each individual assessed themselves and then wrote down comments about each member of the senior team. I then collated these results and gave each person the comments of their colleagues: each individual was then asked to compare their own self-assessment with the assessment of others. I asked each of them to identify a couple of things they are now going to do as a result of these comments.

The consequence of this process is that the members of the senior team are much more overtly committed to each other's success. They now readily prepare papers that are cross-cutting and are willing to accept constructive support and challenge. In discussions on strategic items there is now a strong sense of being committed to each other's success. Once they are away from strategic items they sometimes tend to revert to type – but they recognise this and are determined to take forward a more corporate approach. It is so obvious that people in the organisation notice when they are supportive of each other and when they are less supportive.

When Praesta Partners was set up, a framework was created which helped ensure we would be committed to each other's success. For the individual partners there is no salary: they have equal shares in the partnership and therefore equal shares in the financial return. There is no personal advantage to the person winning a piece of work to do it themselves. This has led to a culture of sharing coaching assignments effectively across the partnership and bringing partners in where their expertise is going to be most valuable.

It is worth asking on a regular basis:

- Are we committed to each other's success?
- How are we showing that we are committed to each other's success? Is this clearly demonstrated both in terms of encouragement, challenge and support?
- Is there more we can do to demonstrate that we are committed to each other's success?

Forgiveness as a value

We talk about stretching targets and clear outcomes: organisations put a lot of work into risk analysis. The best of organisations provide coaching support for individuals to enable them to deliver their outcomes, but how forgiving are we when things go badly?

Organisations will often say that they do not have a 'blame culture' and will give apparent support to those working through particular difficulties. What frequently happens is that a year later those individuals are no longer on the scene; other reasons have been found to move them on. Perhaps this is inevitable.

A crucial test of the integrity of any organisation or individual is how much they are willing to show generosity of spirit. It isn't a matter of forgiving everything, all the time, but it is about enabling people to learn from mistakes and build new capability. A crucial test for an organisation or individual in living their values is about the degree of forgiveness it will allow. If there is no forgiveness the values have no meaning. If there is oft-repeated forgiveness, the vision is likely to have no substance.

It is worth reflecting on:

- How far are you willing to forgive others when they make mistakes?
- How strong a focus do you put on coaching and mentoring so that people can build on the experiences of things that have not gone wrong?
- How willing are you to forgive a boss who lets you down?
- How willing are you to forgive yourself when you make mistakes?
- Have you effective learning mechanisms for coping with your own mistakes and moving on from them?

The values of love and hate

We avoid the word love in a work situation and reserve it for our family and friends. We are more comfortable using the language of trust and respect, and sometimes even affection. In his book *A Lifetime in a Race*, Matthew Pinsent talks of his partnership with Steve Redgrave. It was based on mutual respect and shared challenges. There is a very interesting passage in which this tough, successful rower talks of a love bond that did exist between this successful Olympic duo. There was something special about their partnership which was more than just respect.

The most successful partnerships in a work context will involve more than just trust and respect. There is a sense of upholding and enabling somebody else which will involve a giving of support and encouragement. If selfless giving is at the heart of love in a friendship, then successful working relationships need an element of that love: a strong mutual support enables people to do their job ever more effectively.

An acquaintance was frustrated in many of her relationships with family and at work. I took a risk and reflectively asked whether she let people love her enough. This was overstating the question in order to help her reflect. It was clearly a defining moment. It led to serious conversations at home and at work which meant she became much more relaxed in her own situation and therefore was able to accept the advice of others more readily and also influence them more effectively.

Just as love is a word we do not use in a work context, hate is a word we do not use, but the emotion can sometimes be engendered. The organisation that encourages positive dislike of other organisations may think that it is helping to motivate people. The danger is that it blinkers them so much that their view of the competition ceases to be objective and undermines a true appreciation of the best way of coping with a strong opposition.

After the British Lions lost the first Rugby Union Test in New Zealand in June 2005 the criticism reported in the newspapers was that 'the British Lions didn't hate the New Zealand All Blacks as much as the All Blacks hated the Lions.' New Zealand went on to win all the Tests, with hate rather than with mutual respect colouring the series. Engendering hate was clearly not the way to turn failure into success.

The way we communicate what is important to us can demonstrate our values in a negative way. On 21 July 2005, the chief sports correspondent for the *Evening Standard* used emotive language to describe the effect of a fast ball. He wrote 'So where was the Australian captain to be found at 11.30 a.m. today? Lying on the ground with blood pouring from an inch long wound on his face caused by the ruthless bullying of Steve Harmison.' The article is full of rhetoric about aggression and battles and ends with: 'There seemed to be little sympathy when Langer and Ponting took their sickening blows. Indeed the roars which greeted the very next balls they faced made Lords momentarily seem like the Colosseum. Lords has not scented blood like this for 71 years.' Thankfully the theme of stirring hate became much less strong as the Test series progressed.

Our language in a work situation is rarely going to be as explicit as referring to hate and bullying. But maybe we have to test ourselves as to whether our desire to do well turns into unnecessary aggression and hate. The reasons for not going down this way are:

- Business reasons in terms of respecting the opposition in an objective and not an emotional way.
- Recognising that the opposition one day may become allies the next.
- Remembering the values that are most important to you: if integrity is important, then encouraging hate is hardly going to fit with that value.

The importance of the value of self-esteem and not arrogance

Valuing yourself is a crucial part of stabilising yourself before going into difficult situations. The second commandment of Jesus was 'Love your neighbour as yourself'. The injunction to love others was based on loving yourself first.

Loving yourself is not selfish indulgence if it leads to using that as a basis for loving and supporting others. An honest assessment of your own self-esteem depends on:

- Being very clear about the cultural heritage from which you come.
- Having an honest appreciation of your own personal values and what is important to you.
- Acknowledging your strengths in an objective way.
- Celebrating your successes.
- Being able to refer back in times of difficulty to past accomplishments.

This is not about gloating over your achievements. But it is about an honest self-appraisal and recognising the value of self-esteem. Relevant questions are:

- Is my self-esteem consistent with reality?
- Do I underestimate my own strengths?
- Am I confident enough in my own abilities without being arrogant?

Do we value our customers?

Religious leaders know only too well that if they do not value members of the congregation, they will come less often and go elsewhere. If a supermarket doesn't demonstrate that it values its customers they will soon be spending their money in another store. The test of the reaction of the customer is less immediate for some services. You will have no choice but to go to the nearest Accident and Emergency when you need to visit a hospital quickly; someone wanting to talk about their benefit payment may not have much choice about where to go.

The value of respecting the customer is so important in whatever sphere we are in. A recent survey found that 92 per cent of directors believe that customer service markedly affects their company's reputation. But most senior executives are deliberately kept in the dark about the level of complaints that customer-facing staff have to deal with. Jane Simms in the *Director Magazine*, June 2005, describes this as being as much an abuse of employees (routinely described as 'our greatest asset') as it is of customers (allegedly 'at the heart of everything we do'). Sitting in a call centre being constantly berated by customers about the time they have had to wait to be connected cannot do much for employee engagement. She argues that if directors knew the truth they would surely insist that the customer service processes were redrawn to focus on what matters to the customers and to encourage acting on feedback, rather than being centred only around the needs for efficiency and cost reduction.

Key tests for valuing customers are:

- Who are my customers?
- What value do I place upon them?
- Do I know what my customers want?
- How do I rate the value of meeting the demands of customers alongside other priorities?

Drawing on our values to influence

Sometimes it seems ineffectual to believe in a particular value, but there are examples of oaks growing from acorns. The initial resistance from some to smoking in the workplace has led to its virtual absence nowadays. The growing concern about respect for the environment has led to the increased popularity of new products like solar panels.

Gradually political leaders are being influenced by the need to do something about climate change.

The belief in fair trade is not just theoretical. Decisions about which coffee, tea or bananas are bought are beginning to have an influence. Organic products in supermarkets now command 9 per cent of the business; fair trade products could rise to similar levels. Traidcraft and other organisations are having a powerful influence working with leading supermarkets. The 2005 G8 Conference with its decisions about increased aid for Africa was partially a result of an increasing number of people endorsing the value of 'making poverty history'. This is an example where individuals' voices focusing on a particular value can, over time. begin to have an impact.

Baroness Amos is an example of a senior politician who draws on her values to influence others in a positive way. She was born in Guyana and came to the UK as a child. She had a successful career in training and development and management consultancy before becoming a Foreign Office Minister then Secretary of State for International Development and subsequently Leader of the House of Lords. When she came to England she was put in the bottom class; her mother demanded that her children be tested, and she was transferred to the top class. Her parents were always incredibly supportive so she grew up with self-confidence and a strong sense of family and community. The values that came from her family meant that she never felt odd or left out because she was a black child in a white school. That helped to give her the self-belief which would be so important in the future. She has recorded her perspective as:

'We were a family who debated current affairs a lot and I always had a strong sense of internationalism, as well as a belief in social justice and equality ... The secrets of my success are that I am down to earth and good at anticipating difficulties. I like to feel I can change things but I don't have to be at the front of everything, which means I am a team person.' (*Evening Standard*, 21 July 2005)

For Baroness Amos her values have been important drivers to her, drawing particularly from her family background. But it is not all just driven behaviour. She is very clear: 'I'm serious but I have a fun side as well.'

It is worth reflecting on:

• Are there values which are important to us that we want to share with others?

- What are the most effective ways of influencing individuals or organisations about the importance of failures?
- Is 'fun' an element in the way we communicate our values to others?

The importance of a diversity of values

In both personal and organisational lives we sometimes focus on one set of values and dismiss others. In an increasingly diverse world being sensitive to the values of others must be an essential prerequisite of building a strong sense of community within organisations. Many organisations are increasingly aware of the importance of responding to a range of different cultural and religious values. Trying to find common ground and mutual understanding is central to creating organisations that are going to be effective in a global world.

Sometimes we do feel very uncomfortable about the juxtaposition of different sets of values in a public way. Reality television has been a very overt expression of this juxtaposition of values. Andy Duncan is the Channel 4 Chief Executive who defended the programme *Big Brother* as a parable for our times. He identified some of the positive values promoted by it as 'honesty, integrity, constancy and kindness' (*The Times*, 22 June 2005). He said it was television's role to 'build a wider trust in society and the many different lives, faiths and values that make or break it'. He recognised that many people would dismiss *Big Brother* as foul-mouthed and morally degenerate. For Andy Duncan, 'Tolerance and understanding of others – fundamental New Testament values – can only be built on knowledge and respect. Condemnation so often springs from ignorance and fear.' Whatever our views on TV programmes like *Big Brother* Andy Duncan does raise the right questions about:

- Do we understand the values of people and organisations we are working with?
- Are we objective in understanding the impact of those values on their actions?
- In what ways do we respect their values and are clear that we can work with them?
- In what ways are their values so counter to ours that constructive working together or partnership is unlikely?

What happens to your values in a crisis?

The biggest test for values is in a crisis. If an organisation is in the media spotlight does it stick to its values? To what extent do certain standards slip? Can it test itself to see how well it has lived its values? Taking short cuts might appear necessary when a crisis is on. The prevailing wisdom may well be that you have to be utterly pragmatic, but if too many corners are cut it may take quite a time to rebuild those precious values.

The best way of testing to see if the values are going to be robust in a crisis is to rehearse that situation. It is well worth the investment for a team to act out how they would respond in a crisis. It is just as relevant for an individual. Testing out what happens to the dynamics of relationships and the type of decision making in a hypothetical crisis situation can help identify where the risks are and where values and behaviours need to become even more embedded.

What happens to your personal values in a crisis? Are there some that shine through most strongly and others that become less important. Imagine you are in a crisis:

- Which personal values are most important?
- Who will you draw on for objective support and challenge?
- What are your greatest inner resources to enable you to live your values through a crisis?

Fear as an underminer of values

If a particular situation creates a sense of fear in us we will not be as effective as we want. Our values can go out of the window if we feel a sense of panic. Understanding our fears and working within them is a crucial part of being able to live our values effectively in the workplace. The character of an organisation is personified by its senior leaders; if they generate a culture of fear the organisation will soon die. Fear of the unknown or fear of uncertainty can result because of the limits of our experience. The wider our experience of different situations and people, the less is the likelihood of fear being a dominant influence.

Often we are dishonest with ourselves about what we fear and how best we might cope. If we sense the mildest touch of panic the following might be helpful:

- What is making us fearful?

- Is that fear rational? How have we coped in a similar situation before?
- What has worked for us in terms of overcoming that sense of fear in previous situations?
- If we look at tackling a problem step by step, can that apprehension be removed?
- If the fear comes at particular moments of time how can we persuade ourselves that the sense of fear is going to pass (much less easy if it is at 4 a.m.)?
- Can we sometimes box that fear and throw it over the edge of the cliff?
- Is there a trusted individual with whom we can talk about our fears and be reassured about the positive steps we are taking in those difficult situations?

Learning from our fears is a crucial part of embedding our values. Sometimes our fears are irrational: when we look at the objective facts our fears dissipate. On other occasions our fears are based on a strong intuitive sense that all is not well. When we feel that sense of apprehension it is right to begin to test whether something is awry in both the direction and values of the organisation.

The best way to undermine values

The greatest damage to values comes through deceit and manipulation. Trust, either explicit or implicit, is crucial to effective relations at both personal and corporate levels. If there is any suspicion of deceit or manipulation, trust can rapidly evaporate.

I have seen some very sad examples of where an individual has:

- Distorted facts to enhance or protect their own position.
- Deliberately withheld information.
- Represented a piece of work as theirs when it had been done by somebody else.
- Used moral blackmail to try and influence an outcome.
- Painted a false picture of the implications if a decision is not taken.
- Bent the rules in such a way as to blatantly favour their position.

Although these steps have sometimes been to an individual's initial advantage, they have normally come unstuck because people have begun to recognise what is happening. It is particularly sad when these behaviour patterns begin to surface in people with a track record of integrity. It is well worth trying to understand the personal factors that can lead to these distortions of behaviour. Financial worries, excessive stress and drink can have dangerous effects which are often unnoticed for a surprisingly long time.

Living your own values effectively means avoiding actions which leave you open to accusations of deceit or manipulation. When you see these behaviours in others it is about trying to understand why and then talking through with the individual concerned the nature of the impact they are having on others. Sometimes this will lead to blatant denial; on other occasions there will be a gradual sinking in of reality.

The darker side of values

Sometimes values are a strong power for good. Sometimes they can be undermining. For example, an unblinkered loyalty can mean that an individual is blind to changing circumstances. Many people know of situations where they have set a great store by loyalty, but this loyalty has then not been returned by others. Loyalty can be a very powerful motivating force that keeps you focused through difficult situations. But if you are blind to others abusing that loyalty the end result will be resentment.

Similarly, openness is an important value. To be effective it needs to be returned. If an individual's openness is being abused and information freely given used as a basis to undermine someone then the initial honesty will have been counterproductive. The openness in a working relationship has to be tested from time to time to ensure that there continues to be that mutual respect and trust which enables that openness to work effectively. There is a difficult balancing act between creating values which will mean that trust will happen, and testing that the trust is still there.

What if personal and organisational values are in conflict?

Sometimes we are conscious of value sets that don't fit easily between work and home. Sometimes it is a matter of working that through carefully to find a resolution. Mark Hope, writing as Director of External Relations at Shell UK Exploration and Production, was quoted in *By the Skin of Our Teeth*, edited by Clive Morton. He made clear his view is that you cannot have two different value sets, one for home and one for work.

He reflected that you can, of course, behave differently at home compared to work if you choose, but if that means contravening your values in the workplace that's not good for you and, ultimately, not good for your employer either.

Sometimes the situation is more acute, and an individual feels strongly that their personal values and those of the organisation they are working for are in conflict. This could be a fundamental issue if, for example, somebody worked for a cigarette manufacturer and then decided that smoking was so damaging that they did not want to stay working in the industry. At a different level it could be that an individual working in local government finds him or herself working for politicians who are of a different political complexion. In this case, if such an individual sees as their prime value public service, then it is perfectly possible for them to work for political masters with a range of different persuasions.

Fundamental issues arise for people if a boss asks them:

- To do something that is illegal.
- To take forward action that is unethical (e.g. misrepresenting facts).
- To present a perspective in a very one-dimensional way that borders on the untrue.
- To delay decisions to such a point that it puts a customer or client in a very difficult situation.
- To take actions that are contrary to personal values.

If values are being stretched in a way that you find uncomfortable, then potential steps include:

- Talking with a senior manager explicitly about the issue against the background of the organisation's declared policies or values.
- Being explicit about where the boundary issues seem to lie.
- Talking with a colleague from another part of the organisation who might be able to provide a wider perspective.
- Talking with a friend outside the organisation who understands your value set.

The growing attention being given to business ethics enables individuals to examine the interrelation between their personal values and those of the organisation they work for in a more positive way than was perhaps the case a few years ago. The high profile of the Institute of Business Ethics is evidence of this increased focus. In its publication, *Setting the*

Tone: Ethical Business Leadership, Philippa Foster Back describes some of the tensions that can exist between differing sources of values:

- society, through the legislative process,
- individuals, through their personal values,
- professional bodies and the norms they set, and
- companies themselves which lay down codes of ethics for their staff to follow.

She suggests that the crucial challenge is building trust. She describes the five attributes of an ethical business leader as openness, fair-mindedness, honesty, the ability to listen and having courage. She describes the five key behaviours of such an ethical leader as:

- be open minded and cultivate themselves and others through a willingness to learn,
- be independent and willing to stand up and be counted: challenge the status quo,
- be aware and know that doing the right thing is the right thing to do,
- be considerate and cautious in managing expectations, and
- be determined and direct without fear of confrontation: actively stamping out poor behaviour.

It is worth reflecting on:

- How important is it to you to be regarded as an ethical business leader?
- How independent-minded should you be: in what situations would you be willing to stand up and be counted?
- How best do you balance being 'determined and direct' with being 'considerate and cautious'?
- How would you test whether your sense of the 'right thing to do' is correct?

The impact of values when starting a new job

It is particularly relevant to look at your values when you start a new job. They can help guide your priorities and your personal impact.

James was about to start a new job as a board member for a major national organisation and reflected on the values that were going to be most important to him in this new role. He was very clear in his prospectus. He describes his five values in the following way:

- Hard edge: encouraging people to excel and be their best and be seen to be their best. He wants to encourage people to bring clear thinking on specific issues, to work collectively in a disciplined way to deliver objectives and to be ready to take tough decisions.
- Humanity: this is about caring for people and recognising the importance of work/life balance. It is a focus on each person being different and needing to be treated fairly.
- Humility: key themes here are listening and learning. It is important to learn from everyone including those who work for you. There is a need to develop a sense of not being irreplaceable whilst being adaptable to take on new roles.
- Honesty: openness, communication and trust are central with a clear expectation that people are completely honest and frank.
- Humour: retaining a perspective, celebrating success and creating times where there is laughter and fun. Humour is part of retaining a perspective and seeing the job in hand as part of wider horizons: the job itself should not be the be-all and end-all but part of a wider satisfaction in the richness of living.

For James these values came out of his own personal experience and learning. They reflected the essential 'James-ness'. He is trying to balance what matters most to him as an individual, what comes out of his personal experience, and how best the business to be done can be delivered. Did hard edge come first or last? He concluded it was right that it came first because the organisation has to deliver its outcomes for people to have jobs. But the way the business delivers its objectives depends crucially on the other values too. James was adamant that there should be a synergy between his personal values and the values he wants to espouse within the organisation. For James living these values depends on:

- being very clear about them at the start,
- ensuring people give him feedback,
- honestly assessing his effectiveness in living these values,
- being willing to learn and change in the light of experience, and
- keeping utter objectivity in assessing how well he is doing in living these values.

There may be useful parallels here when starting any new role.

Clarifying your values

Sometimes I encourage people to write down their four core values and what they mean to them. This simple and quick exercise provides a very good framework for discussion about where these values come from, how they influence their life and work, and how they want to develop the values further. Reflecting quickly and articulating first thoughts about values can be so helpful for an individual in illustrating what is most important to them. A more comprehensive approach is to go through the following steps.

- What have been the strongest influences shaping my values
  - family
  - culture
  - community
  - faith
  - education?
- What have been the strongest values resulting from these influences?
- Which are the four most important values in this list?
- Then look very closely at each value, possibly spending the spare moments in one day reflecting on one of the values and then going through the same process on a different day with another of the values.
- What does the value mean to you?
- How has this value been relevant to you in particular situations?
- Is the value standing the test of time – does it need to evolve?
- Does the value resonate with the values of the organisations of which you are part?
- Then look at your set of four values:
  - Are they a complete picture?
  - Are they robust enough for the future?
  - Would the following people recognise your living these values: family, friends, neighbours, your staff, peers and your boss?
- What changes (if any) would you want to make to these values?
- With whom will you share your renewed intention to live by this set of values?
- How will you hold yourself to account for living these values?

Another approach is to look through a possible list of values and to decide which four:

- you resonate with most,

- you would like to reinforce in yourself,
- you would like to help grow in organisations of which you are part, and
- you want to particularly celebrate in others.

Here is an illustrative list of values:

trust	integrity
openness	innovation
honesty	loyalty
boldness	companionship
rigour	security
courage	respect
creativity	order
initiative	partnership
happiness	passion
persistence	quality
frankness	fulfilment
commitment	purposefulness
friendship	self-control
dependability	joyfulness
delivery	stewardship
service	success
fairness	determination
diversity	encouragement
justice	character
profitability	responsiveness
learning	adventure
clarity	foresight
sincerity	compassion
humour	forgiveness
adaptability	cooperation
recognition	kindness
resolve	warmth
conviction	transparency
single-mindedness	professionalism

After you have identified a number of key values for yourself it is worth reflecting on:

- Why have I chosen these?
- Are they a mixture of 'hard' and 'soft' values?

- Would other people recognise these values in me?
- What next in terms of embedding these values?
- What values were near misses in my final list and why did I exclude them?

Are values important?

It is perfectly possible to do a job in a utilitarian way where there is no particular emphasis on values, but a focus on values can enrich the quality of relationships within an organisation and therefore its effectiveness. For the junior members of staff to understand the values of an organisation and see themselves as a part of the overall whole can have a powerful effect on their motivation. And to the extent that values are important to leaders within an organisation it is contradictory not to try and cultivate an atmosphere within the organisation where individual values are appreciated. Values are not soft, wet management. They are about enabling people to do the toughest of jobs fairly and equitably.

Suma Chakrabarti, in his role as Permanent Secretary at the Department for International Development, talks about his firm belief in the mission of this organisation. He believes strongly in the importance of honesty, transparency and openness: 'it is crucial never to cloud the key issues but to be very frank and open about them'. He has a strong belief in recognising individual merit. His values come from his experience of life in India. When he visited India at the age of 10 after a few years away and saw the poverty there, it focused him on the value of over-coming poverty and enabling people to progress on the basis of individual merit.

When he felt that certain values were being belittled he said he felt grubby. He was clear that there were limits beyond which he would not go. As he had grown in experience the red line had become redder: he had become more at peace with himself in terms of living his values. His advice to others is this: 'Whatever you do, you need to stay with your values and be able to laugh at yourself.'

Some key issues to reflect on in terms of living your values:

- What are the key values that are most important to you?
- How consistently do you live those values?
- Are those values changing? Do you want them to change?

- Are your values consistent with your vision and how you want to add value?
- How can you embed the values that are most important to you in the way you impact on your colleagues even more?

Chapter 4:

Value-added

The fruit of the Spirit is love, joy, peace, patience, kindness, goodness, faithfulness, gentleness and self-control.

Galatians, Chapter 5

Value-added has become a popular phrase. It is used in education to refer to the added value a particular phase of education builds on a previous phase. It is used in business and commerce to refer to the benefits of a particular stage in a business process. The definition of value-added used in the chapter is 'bringing a distinctive contribution that makes a significant difference to personal or organisational outcomes'.

Looking at value-added is an ideal way of standing back and reflecting on what the distinctive contribution is that each individual can bring. Our individual value-added will change over time: it will be different in different situations. Applying a test of value-added rigorously will mean that we vary our contribution depending on the context. If our style and approach is always the same it is likely that we are not adding value in the most productive way. Widening our repertoire in the way we add value is one of the most powerful things we can do.

Each role adds value in a different way. The ticket inspector, footballer, researcher, teacher and politician are all concerned to add value. For some it is instant. The footballer who scores a goal is adding value very visibly: the celebration of the fans reflects the pleasure of the achievement. The researcher is bringing value-added more slowly and steadily. The true benefits of the research will only be seen well after the researcher has completed the work and the results have become embedded in policy change. The results of the work of the teacher as they add value will only be fully seen a decade or so later when the child has grown into an adult.

Each of these examples of value-added depend on careful, thorough preparation. The footballer who scores the goal adds value in an instant because he has practised and trained over many hours. Politicians add value when they identify changes in needs or expectations and influence the way legislation is enacted or resources focused. A ticket collector adds value by selling tickets and through acting as a deterrent to avoiding payment, adding value by the way the job is done and ensuring that travelling on a train is a pleasant experience. A grumpy ticket collector can turn a journey into an unpleasant experience.

This chapter looks at themes such as:

- Different ways of adding value.
- Value-added that changes over time.
- The relationship between value-added at personal and corporate levels.
- Adapting different approaches to developing your value-added contribution.
- Bringing together different strands of your value-added contribution.

Different ways of adding value

These illustrations demonstrate the variety of ways in which we can add value. For example it can be through:

- Providing a specific crucial piece of specialist information.
- Bringing a specialist skill that provides a perspective or takes a particular task onto another stage.
- Enabling a group of people to work together.
- Seeing clearly the next steps and giving some direction to a discussion or a piece of work.
- Identifying very clearly the outcomes that are necessary.
- Providing the encouragement and goodwill that enables people to work together effectively.
- Enabling individuals to learn and grow through the experiences that they are going through.

We may have very different means of adding value in different groups:

- in some groups we may be the specialist,

- in other groups we may provide clarity about the way forward,
- in some groups we may provide the emotional glue, and
- in others we may be the one who is able to crystallise the learning that is going on.

Sometimes within the same activity or within the same team we may provide a different value-added at different stages:

- at the start we may be the one who sets a particular group in a specific direction,
- we might then delegate responsibility to somebody else and become an adviser, and
- later we may be purely an observer providing encouragement for those still involved in this particular enterprise.

Some of the key tests for us are:

- How good are we at assessing when we can add most value?
- How good are we at evolving the way we add value to take account of changing needs and circumstances?
- Do we mind if the value we are able to give drops dramatically because good progress is being made by others?
- Can we withdraw gracefully when there is no need for us to continue to contribute?

Being clear how to add value

Sometimes we think of the way we add value in a rather narrow way. If an individual's experience has been in marketing they will probably describe themselves as a marketing expert. That is a highly specific way in which they have added value. But their skills might actually be wider than that. Their value-added contribution may be more about creative problem solving, with marketing being an example of that skill. Sometimes we can limit ourselves by defining our value-added in a rather narrow way.

Someone might describe themselves as being in the food and beverage industry which limits, in many people's minds, the contribution they can bring in other spheres. But their value-added may well have been delivering major change in a complex commercial situation. That value-added skill is transferable to many different situations. Looking at the way we add value in a generic way can open up exciting new horizons and enable us to move on into new and different spheres. What follows are two examples of leaders who are clear about the way they are seeking to add value.

Ken Boston, the Chief Executive of the Qualifications and Curriculum Authority, is very candid that the main value-added that he can bring is 'The ability to say what I mean clearly and directly and without offence.' His focus is being the 'plain man's plain man'. He is rigorous in the economy with which he uses words. His focus is on nouns and verbs and not adjectives or adverbs. This mean his conclusions are clear without elaboration. He says that:

> 'The heart of adding effective value is to be constantly alert and aware of changing attitudes or reactions. If there is something surprising seek it out: your intuitive judgement will indicate whether there might be an issue. Sometimes adding value is very deliberate and conscious: if somebody is struggling they will need your support. If work becomes a bit scrappy, your focus is needed to ensure value-added quality is maintained. Sometimes big issues appear on the radar and it falls inevitably to the Chief Executive to take the initiative. Some things cannot be delegated: it has to be the Chief Executive who provides the thinking, the strategic direction and persuades key interlocutors. Sometimes the added value comes as much through the position of Chief Executive as through the individual in that role. It has to be the Chief Executive that interrelates with the Secretary of State. But on many other occasions the value-added can be achieved by people who are much more junior in the organisation.'

For Ken, a key part of the value-added contribution of the CEO is being intuitive, being brave, and taking a risk and backing yourself. 'Experience will have provided both knowledge and insights that are explicit and intuitive. The good Chief Executive is adapting to their environment but then reaching a focused view with the ability to say what you mean clearly and directly and without offence.'

Jean is reflective about the way she has added value as a managing director. She said that when she started this role she was probably rather naive: she assumed that she just had to say what she wanted and it happened. What had became increasingly clear to her was the need to communicate effectively either individually or through groups. She could only add value effectively if she used communication to influence key people in a variety of ways. She was adding value in different ways with different people: some needed clear direction and others needed a more general steer. Her perspective was:

- If you understand somebody's personality type it enables you to respond more clearly to their leadership needs.
- It was when she understood what somebody's comfort zone was that she was better able to identify development needs which, when addressed, enabled value to be added more effectively.
- The great challenge of leadership is identifying abilities and finding the right way of stretching people so that their value-added can grow.

How do we want our value-added to change over time?

We add value in different ways at different stages of our lives. For example:

- a junior doctor adds value by being immediately available to help in a wide variety of ways,
- the medical consultant adds value through their leadership of individual operations,
- the medical specialist, who has very wide experience, will be adding value through leading the research and professional development, and
- the wise medical consultant will add value through the tuition given to junior doctors.

In this illustration, and in many different examples, we add value in different ways at different stages of our lives – which comes full circle as we mentor and encourage others.

Being utterly objective about how we add value now and then asking how we want to add value in the future is an exercise that is well worthwhile. If the way we add value now depends on a high level of energetic commitment we may not be able to sustain that for the rest of our lives. Growing in experience and wisdom enables us to contribute just as effectively but in different ways. The best of leaders are able to do that taking account of their changing skills and preferences and the needs of those around them. Planning ahead for the way we want to add value in the future is always worthwhile. For example:

- As a young manager with lots of energy it is worth experimenting with how you can use your energy the more effectively to be ready for when your energy levels become less.

- You may not have family responsibilities now but one day you may well want to be at home by 6.30 p.m. to spend time with your children, therefore learning to use your time management skills effectively is a good investment.
- Increasing your understanding of IT is always going to be a good investment.
- If in due course you want to be able to manage a group of people, then taking the opportunity for some management experience at an early stage can be invaluable.
- If you know that in a future role you will have to give public presentations, then doing one or two now would help give you the confidence to do more in the future.

Planning to develop your value-added skills is not only about what you do in a work environment. It is looking across the whole of your life to see how learning skills in one area of your life can feed across into other areas. For example:

- There may not be much opportunity in your current role for chairing meetings, but maybe you can offer to do that in the community group of which you are part.
- You may feel nervous about standing up in public and talking; to help allay those nerves could you offer to take a lead in something like your local church, mosque or sports club.
- It might be useful to develop mentoring skills for a future role: perhaps you could offer to mentor a sixth former at the local college or an overseas student at the local university.

Preparing ourselves for the way we add value is never going to be wasted. My mother used to tell the story of her father, who was an office boy in a woollen mill in Huddersfield. At his own initiative he had been learning French at night school. One day there was a visitor from Europe: the mill manager sent a message round to ask if anybody could read French fluently and translate something. My grandfather volunteered to translate the text, built a good relationship with the mill manager and was soon moving through a sequence of management positions before eventually becoming the mill manager himself. He had developed his confidence and his abilities to speak French in such a way that one day he had an opportunity to apply that skill, which brought him recognition and advancement.

John Dunford is clear that he adds value in a different way now, as General Secretary of the Association of School and College Leaders, than he did as a head teacher. He cannot be involved in the same level of detail and has to take a bigger-picture view. Because he is constantly away from his office he has to rely on those back at the ASCL office to deal with the day-to-day business. When he was away on holiday for three weeks one summer, a major issue blew up about Key Stage 3 results. His deputy took a clear lead on this and has been the one taking the lead on this particular subject ever since.

John talks of the importance of adaptability in terms of the added value he brings. The Association has a President who is elected for a one-year term. It is crucial that the President and the General Secretary operate in a complementary way. They agree priorities for the year ahead at the start of each presidency. If the President is a curriculum expert, for instance, then John will focus on other areas. It is crucial that there is a clear mutual understanding about where each person is going to add value. Because of busy schedules the President and the General Secretary pass 'like ships in the night'. Telephone and email contact is so important. For John email is wonderful in ensuring the most effective teamwork.

He has thought hard about how he adds value. The key priorities for the Association are determined by its policy committees, and this provides John with the framework within which he can operate. His value-added comes from how he takes forward the policy. He defines his particular value as:

- Doing what other people cannot do through using his network of educational and political contacts.
- Using short conversations to the best possible effect to listen and to influence.
- Keeping up a professionalism that is rooted in his experience as a school teacher so that there is always the 'street cred' of his professional background.
- Always seeing himself in other people's shoes so that he understands their perspective.
- Always being clear about the implementation aspects of any policy, on the basis that policies are useless unless they can be implemented.

He uses his considerable energy to add value at key points through knowing the right people, knowing how to influence people and communicating the Association's policies effectively in a wide range of different contexts.

John Dunford is a superb example of keeping a strong focus on how he adds value and then adapting his approach to meet particular circumstances. Key reflections from this are:

- How readily can we sit ourselves in someone else's shoes and see how we can add most value for them?
- How willing are we to flex the way we add value to meet different situations and the needs of different individuals?
- Are we willing to countenance completely different ways of adding value if requested to do so?

How do we want to stretch the way in which we add value?

We develop the way we add value through:

- building on our strengths, and
- developing new competences in areas which may not have been our previous strengths.

If somebody is a good oral communicator, then building on that strength is an important way of strengthening their value-added. Even the good communicator can learn more about the best way of holding people's attention and influencing them. Moving into a bigger leadership role does not mean leaving your strengths behind. It means building on them in the most effective way. If the 'essential Charlie-ness' has been an effective part of an individual's leadership in terms of the way they motivate others it is crucial that this ability is not diluted through promotion. It may need to be channelled in different ways but it should not be squashed.

Often strengths in one job become liabilities in another. The individual who is an excellent project manager and can get things done will have achieved a great deal, but in a more senior post the temptation to do things themselves may undermine the people who are working for them. There are often going to be step changes in competences and attitudes that are necessary when moving from one job to another. The great skill is to identify clearly what changes are needed in somebody's approach and then for the individual to work carefully on developing a wider suite of competences and approaches. The most obvious example of this is about delegation where the senior manager, both to survive and to motivate staff, must delegate effectively.

David Adleman talks of the step change in the value-added contribution he aims to bring as principal of a college. As a head of department the management responsibilities are clear. As principal, creating a single community where the principal is accessible and approachable is your responsibility. You have to be good at:

- bringing the best out of your staff,
- leading consultation formally and informally so that you understand people's attitudes,
- taking people with you when unpalatable decisions have to be taken,
- ensuring a strategic approach across the whole college, and
- ensuring there is a holistic thinking which links together decisions about the overall budget with the wellbeing of individual subject areas.

The value-added has to be based on a good understanding of how teaching and learning fit together. There has to be a clear understanding of the whole institution in terms of its strengths and the weaknesses of different systems. You have to add value in areas that previously, as a head of department, you never really needed to get involved in such as leading on major development or building projects. For David a crucial ingredient of adding value as principal is keeping abreast of changing wider developments which include:

- taking a careful interest in the way education policy is developing,
- being aware of initiatives in other similar institutions,
- reading and taking an interest in public policy debates, and
- being clear where his intellectual interest and moral commitment lay.

The job of the principal is not just about individual problem solving, it is about seeing a bigger picture that is concerned with political and ethical realities. There are clear parallels for leaders in a range of spheres. David's approach, for example, is just as relevant to leaders in health, social work or local government.

It is worth reflecting on how we want to stretch the value-added contribution we bring. It may be forced upon us by promotion, a new job or very different customers:

- Are we open to stretching the value-added contribution we bring?
- Can we see how we want to stretch it further?

Learning from how others add value

Observing how someone else adds value is a powerful way of learning at work. If you ever have the opportunity to work-shadow somebody whom you respect, watch how they use their time and their words. Talk with them in advance about what they want to get out of particular meetings and how they are approaching them; recap with them afterwards about what has gone well and what has gone less well. Sometimes people find it difficult to explain in detail why they chose different approaches, but often putting them on the spot and asking them directly will help them in articulating how they are trying to add value in different ways in different situations. When observing somebody closely, the key questions to ask yourself are:

- What did I most appreciate about the way they used their time?
- What did I learn from their approach in particular discussions?
- What two things do I particularly want to build into my own style of working having observed this person?
- What would I do differently?

Helen described how work-shadowing somebody for a day helped her to focus on:

- how to network more effectively,
- when to contribute to a meeting and when to stay silent,
- when to signal the need to move on, and
- when to try and force a discussion to conclusion.

You might think that work-shadowing somebody is an imposition on them. Most people find they benefit from somebody who work-shadows them: it is like having free consultancy advice. If somebody you work-shadow asks for feedback, always give it and be honest. That is their payoff for letting you work-shadow them.

Another way of learning from others is to be mentored. Jean, who has just turned 40, talks of the importance of 'getting a mentor or three'. This was her strongest recommendation to a group of aspiring middle managers. She said that mentors at crucial stages of her career had helped to give her the confidence to do well and helped her focus on the key next steps. She keeps in touch with those people who have mentored her. It is clear that entering a two-way mentoring relationship can be of great help to both people.

Complementing others in the way you add value

One of the key questions for leaders is how they add value to their team. You might be particularly good at a certain activity, but if one of your team is strong in that skill it would be a waste of your time to spend a lot of your energy on that specific activity yourself. Having an absolutely objective view about the skills of your team and where you can best add value is one of the greatest secrets of success. The best leaders are always flexing the way they add value, responding to different situations, taking account of the strengths of their team and the perspectives of different stakeholders.

It may well be that your value-added as leader of a team will differ markedly in relation to different team members. John, a senior executive in a manufacturing industry, had just been given two additional business areas. He now had two completely different team leaders. With one he needed to be clear about strategy on the way ahead and set a clear direction, and with the other it was much more gentle steering that was needed; if he had tried to set a precise direction he would have been put firmly back in his place. He wondered whether this diversity of approach was right, but the more he reflected on it the more it became clear that a markedly different approach was just what was needed to bring the best out of these two colleagues, who both had great strengths.

Balancing vision and values

Leadership at its best brings together a focus on both vision and values to help ensure clarity about bringing value-added most effectively. The best sort of value-added comes when there is clarity about direction and outcomes, coupled with a warm heart and a generosity of spirit which provides support and encouragement.

How do you rate yourself on that balance between clarity of direction and strength of emotional support? It might be worth ranking the following:

- The strength of your intellectual leadership.
- The pragmatism of your focus on delivery.
- The warmth of your support and encouragement.
- The depth of your understanding of how people in key relationships work.
- Your grasp of how best to deliver change.

Ranking these means of value-added can give an indication of the strengths to build on, where you need to develop and the complementary skills that you need in your team.

A good example of a leader who brought both a clear sense of vision and a generous heart is Sandy Millar, who spent twenty years as Vicar of Holy Trinity, Brompton. With eight new church plants, a totally renovated main site, a quadrupled congregation and new ministries with the poor and dispossessed, his role radically changed. In recent years the Alpha initiative has resulted in courses about the Christian faith worldwide. What was the particular value-added that Sandy Millar brought? He arrived as a young curate in 1976 and brought a boldness to innovate with an intense desire to preserve unity. Comments from others about the value-added he brought include the following:

- 'He has led with remarkable perception, wisdom, drive and diplomacy.'
- 'His generosity, graciousness and servant heartedness combine with his clear sense of vision, determined perseverance and purpose.'
- 'He has an unparalleled ability to make everyone feel loved.'
- 'He is a man of great warmth. He is insightful and inspirational.'

The Archbishop of Canterbury summed up his value-added: 'Sandy is someone whose skill in communicating the Gospel is bound up with being supremely and happily himself – never a prisoner of the institution or of other people's fantasies, but free before God.' Whether or not faith is important to you, Sandy is an example of value-added leadership that is both visionary and inspirational but also warm and generous hearted. It is an example that effective value-added leadership is not about dogmatism or inflexibility but about building the right climate for change and ensuring a whole range of different people are inspired and motivated to act together with a shared vision.

Link between values and value-added for both organisations and individuals

There ought to be a clear link between values and value-added. A good example of this is the approach taken by the Department for Constitutional Affairs (DCA). This Department was set up to deliver justice, rights and democracy for the public covering areas like courts, legal aid and constitutional change. In May 2005 it published a set of priorities under the title 'Making a Difference: Taking Forward Our Priorities'. It started with a strong focus on values. The first subheading was 'What we believe'. This was summed up in the following words:

'Our priorities are the public's priorities. People want their legal and democratic systems to be respected for their values of fairness, decency and opportunity for all. They want judges and courts that are independent and effective at delivering justice. They want the rule of law upheld. They want lawyers who give decent and transparent advice for a fair price.'

The rest of the document is a clear statement of how the DCA wants to add value to enable the values of fairness, decency and opportunity for all to be fully expressed. The document talks about:

- Creating a fairer deal for the tax payer on the use of legal aid.
- Giving better support to the 28,000 magistrates who give their time to deliver the justice that often has the biggest impact on the quality of life in local communities.
- Bringing to justice a higher proportion of those people who breach court orders on bail, community penalties and fines.
- Improving the practical support that jurors receive.
- Increasing the diversity of the judiciary.

The thrust of this document was how the DCA could add value in a way which allowed courts, magistrates, judges and jurors to add their value in the most effective way. This illustration shows the importance of looking at added value through a sequence of steps:

- How could Parliament add value to enable the DCA to do its job?
- How could the DCA bring most added value to the judges and the courts?
- How could the courts bring the most effective value-added to magistrates and jurors in doing their jobs?
- How can judges, magistrates and jurors do their job in relation to considering crimes in the most value-added way?

Looking at the different steps in a value-added process is just as important at the individual level.

- How does the head teacher best add value to the head of department who is then going to provide the best value-added they can for the classroom teacher whose role is developing the competences and skills of the student?

- How does the hospital administrator enable the medical consultant to work most effectively, thus enabling the junior doctors to make their contributions effectively, and drawing on the skills of the nurses in the best possible way so that the patient receives high-quality treatment?
- How does the factory manager add most value to the production manager who is drawing out the skills of the foremen in their utilising the dexterity and experience of the workers on the shop floor, all in order to produce the best quality product for the customer?

Relationship between corporate and personal value-added

Both for an organisation's success and an individual's fulfilment there needs to be a synergy between the value-added of what the organisation is trying to do and the value-added of the individual within it. There is a natural synergy in a hospital between the objective of the hospital, in terms of improving people's health, and the role of an individual doctor within it. There is a parallel situation in an educational institution where the objectives of the university or the lecturer are normally consistent with each other. In a large commercial organisation there may be a number of steps between the value-added nature of the organisation and that of an individual. A bank is concerned about maximising the return on investment. An individual employee may be measuring their value-added in terms of ensuring an effective building project, developing the skills of individual members of staff or ensuring an effective IT system is in place.

Suma Chakrabarti, Permanent Secretary of the Department for International Development (DFID), gave a speech in November 2004 to all members of the senior civil service within that Department emphasising the importance of strong leadership. He talked about the following strengths of the organisation:

- The strong personal commitment of members of the Department to the mission of the organisation to eliminate global poverty.
- The strength of leadership on development strategy and the ability to challenge traditional thinking and rebut attempts to dilute the Department's mission.
- The intellectual authority and technical competence in the international development system.

Suma was clear that DFID needed to become better at managing change and building greater emotional resilience in the face of change. The value-added he wanted to encourage within the organisation was that, as senior members of staff, we:

- must become more proactive, less reactive, in setting priorities and in providing clear direction,
- need to act more as corporate leaders than as champions for a particular part of DFID or for individual staff members,
- must become more decisive and have the courage of our convictions based on our experience,
- must achieve closure more quickly and stick to the agreed line,
- must take greater personal responsibility for decisions,
- must articulate the change agenda day in, day out,
- need to up our game further on performance management,
- should do more to plan for and coach the next generation of potential leaders,
- should listen to the feedback and help take the strain with our staff as changes are implemented, and
- should support each other more visibly and vocally.

He was linking together the value-added of DFID with the value-added he wanted to see develop in its senior leaders. It is significant that this list is much more about managing change and building emotional intelligence and resilience than it is about specific technical skills. Many of the leaders in DFID already had strong technical expertise. The value-added that Suma was encouraging them to bring was about communication, decisiveness, personal responsibility, listening, coaching and support for each other. The success of this approach is evident from the high esteem in which DFID has been held within government and within the wider development world.

Andrew Higginson, the Tesco Finance and Strategy Director, stresses the importance of recognising your strengths and weaknesses. He emphasises the importance of giving airtime to the things you are not so keen on, and disciplining yourself in the things you are not so good at. You cannot duck the areas where you need to add value. He sees as his particular areas of adding value:

- steering his people,
- bringing on his staff and mentoring them, and
- always bringing a different perspective in discussion with his peers.

Andrew is very conscious that there must be alignment between how Tesco expects him to bring value-added as Finance and Strategy Director and his personal value-added contribution as a director and board member.

A key issue when working in any organisation is clarity about your understanding of what value-added the organisation wants of you and what value-added contribution you want to bring. Key tests are:

- Is what the organisation wants of you what you want and feel able to give?
- Can you adapt your value-added to meet the most important needs within the organisation?
- Is this an opportunity to stretch your contribution into new areas such as mentoring?

Value-added in an area outside your expertise

You might be asked to make a contribution in a new area that is outside your own area of experience. It might be in a very different department or with very different people. It is worth thinking laterally about what you might bring to the task which complements the skills of those already working in that area. You might bring:

- some technical skills they lack,
- networks that might be useful,
- a wider perspective,
- a different way of looking at issues, or
- the ability to build partnership and teams.

It is often worth thinking about how you will build credibility in a new sphere in a measured way. There is no need to panic! There is always a distinctive contribution you can make. In my career within government, the job I enjoyed most was as a Regional Director in the north-east of England. My previous background had been in the Department of Education and the Treasury. The Regional Director role was mainly concerned with inner-city policy, environmental issues and transport: I had no background in these areas. What was relevant was the background I had in working with Ministers, a range of different partners and Central Government Departments. The value-added I aimed to bring was not about the detail of the subject but about a wider perspective and the building of key relationships.

If you are approaching a new job in a very different organisation try to reflect on the generic skills that are relevant. Mastering some of the detail will be important, but key questions are:

- What wider perspective can I bring to this role?
- What type of generic skills are going to be relevant (e.g. marketing, project management, team building)?
- What networks can I bring that will be relevant to this role?
- What are the gaps in the current team where I can bring a particular perspective?
- How can I provide mentoring in the skills that I bring?

Parallels can be drawn from the sporting world. Duncan Fletcher helped bring success to the England cricket team. He provides leadership as a coach which was not based on having played Test cricket. Duncan Fletcher's golden rules, quoted in the *Sunday Times* of 26 June 2005, are in terms of value-added leadership:

- Joint leaders don't work: if two individuals are in positions of authority, ensure that their roles are clearly defined and that ultimate decision-making power rests with just one of them.
- Never be afraid to hand responsibility to people: have faith in human nature. Don't try to dictate to people. Give them a chance to prove themselves and to learn from their mistakes. They will rarely let you down.
- Co-opt the rebellious by awarding them management responsibility: don't just sit there getting irritated by people who won't subscribe to a team ethic. If their ability makes them worth keeping, give them management responsibility and watch their characters change.
- Listen to what your team is telling you: there is nothing more de-motivating than a manager who won't listen. Your people will more than likely know their own job better than you do. So if they're telling you something, it might be worth taking heed.
- Always be sensitive to the human balance of your team: team spirit is a vital ingredient for success. Take care to ensure that your team has a critical mass of individuals who get along with each other and have a team-orientated personality.
- If you show faith in individuals, they will repay you: people will

generally respond to a manager who says that he believes in them and is prepared to work with them over the long term to capitalise on their strengths.

- Commitment from the manager is in itself a motivating force: don't ask your people to put in maximum effort if you are not prepared to do the same. Resentment and cynicism will be the inevitable result. Strong work ethic, on the other hand, can be infectious.
- Only criticise in private: no individual likes to be rebuked in front of others. Arguments in the heat of the moment can escalate, causing irreparable damage to a working relationship. Save your criticism for when you are behind closed doors.
- For every action there is a reaction: always establish the root of a problem. Don't jump in head first to tackle problems in individual or team performance. What you are seeing are the symptoms. You constantly need to ask why something is happening and then address that.
- Recruit character: it's very difficult to change mental make-up. It's much easier to improve technical faults or to teach new skills so as to transform an individual's personality. Ensure as far as practicable that the person you are recruiting has the right stuff.

Duncan Fletcher's golden rules are just as relevant in a management situation in any sector. They are particularly transferable where you, as leader, do not have the same detailed level of experience as the people you are responsible for.

Value-added through moving out of your comfort zone

Once we have developed particular strengths our natural inclination is to work within those strengths. Building and using our strengths is crucial: in each phase we need to develop a wider repertoire of how we add value. Moving out of our comfort zone can mean such changes as:

- delegating and trusting people more,
- reaching conclusions on limited personal experience,
- being willing to seek to influence a wider range of people at more senior levels,
- coming in and out of subjects and issues for shorter periods and identifying the one or two aspects we think are most important, or

- standing back and seeing the wider context of where particular developments are likely to lead.

If our comfort zone is in one-to-one discussions we may want to experiment with making different types of contributions in groups. We can imagine we are talking to one person within the group as a means of settling ourselves before making contributions. We can be encouraged by those who have experimented outside their comfort zones.

Roger feels very comfortable in small groups but very uncomfortable in groups of above four in size. He often has to play a key role in large groups but is inhibited and therefore not influential. His tendency is to come into the discussion late after the momentum has developed in a particular direction. He therefore tends to come over as defensive. The approach that he decided to adopt is:

- to prepare carefully for larger meetings so that he is sure of his ground,
- to ensure that he sits opposite the Chair so that he feels fully part of the meeting and not on the outside,
- to aim to maintain strong eye contact with the Chair and key players in the discussion,
- to make focused contributions having jotted down some key bullet points,
- to make some contributions early in a discussion to see how much they influence the flow of the meeting, and
- to agree in advance with the Chair if he did want to ensure that he came in early on a particular item.

Through experimenting Roger is becoming much more confident in his contributions in larger meetings when he sees the results of the new approach he is taking. There continue to be some occasions when his nervousness means that he does not have quite the impact he wants. But steadily he is having a much more focused and influential impact on meetings.

Roger's experience is an example of identifying an area where you want to add value and where you have limited confidence at the moment. Roger's approach was to stand back and:

- be objective about what he was less good at and try to understand why,
- be clear about the approaches he was going to use to address this, and
- be willing to experiment using some simple techniques.

Value-added that comes from learning through mistakes

As a coach, the value-added that I can bring to people is more as a result of my failures than my successes. We learn much through the hard reality of our mistakes. The learning only comes when we are completely honest about what has gone well and what has gone less well. A colleague and I used to walk back from the office to Waterloo station in London from time to time and had a discipline of talking about what had gone well and what had gone less well during the day. We mentored each other in terms of what was the learning from things that had gone less well.

One way of reflecting on this is through asking questions like these.

- Over the last week what activities was I involved in that did not go as well as I had hoped?
- What were the reasons for this? Was it because of the actions of others? What can I learn from their mistakes?
- Did it go less well because of an action I took or a contribution I made? Was it still right to have taken that step or in retrospect would I have done it differently?
- What is the learning that I ought now to embed in the way I contribute?
- Am I clear how I am going to hold my nerve and contribute on a future occasion but in a different way?

Additionally, we can learn a great deal by observing how other people respond to mistakes. Are they honest about what has gone wrong: are they over-defensive in the way they react?

Michael Cunnah, as the Chief Executive of Wembley National Stadium Limited, has the job of leading this major infrastructure project. He has had to put up with a lot of criticism but is clear that the scale of the ambition has proved right. On the subject of the early mistakes he commented:

'There is no right way to do this. You are never going to get everything right first time. You learn as you go through. We achieved funding by listening to banks and understanding their requirements. We tailored the project to fit that point of view.'
(*Director Magazine*, July 2005)

There have been some interesting innovations in learning from mistakes. Gerhard Bihl, Head of Personnel and Social Services at BMW Regensburg, started an initiative with the original title of 'Flop of the Month', although it was really about the 'creative error of the month' (*Daily Telegraph*, 16 June 2005). Employees were honoured who had developed ideas and projects, even though they ultimately failed. One recipient was someone who wanted to enable a blind man to work in the manufacturing plant. The employee pursued the project with considerable energy. Sadly the project failed because the blind person felt overwhelmed by the job. The employee who had done all the organising was terrified of the potential reaction of his colleagues. Receiving the 'creative error of the month' award reduced the finger wagging. He was praised for an innovative idea which he had taken forward in a constructive and determined way.

The value-added that a leader brings is significantly related to how they view mistakes. The BMW example illustrates how an individual can be recognised even though their efforts have not worked.

Be ready to be surprised

We can be predictable in our approaches and in our own self-assessment: we can almost predetermine how successful we are going to be by our attitude in approaching a particular situation. If we do not think we are going to be good at doing a major presentation, we are not likely to be that successful.

If we think we are going to fail in an interview we are unlikely to be successful. A key factor in making a success of an interview is believing you can do the job. Effective preparation involves imagining oneself in the job and seeing the joys and successes that being in that role can bring. Once you have fully absorbed what it would be like to be successful in a particular job you can go into an interview in a much more confident way. When the questions come, you as the interviewee, are then addressing them as if you are doing the job successfully. This provides the right confidence to demonstrate that you are likely to be successful in the role.

This approach of imagining yourself being successful applies to any situation that looks as if it is going to be demanding. Imagine being in the role and experiencing the joys and the frustrations. In that way you will be so much better prepared intellectually and emotionally.

Be ready to be surprised about how you will respond to particular situations. If a presentation is well prepared there can be that lift when there is good feedback. What helps for the future is to capture that moment so that the attitude of mind changes from 'I do not look forward to this sort of event' to 'I now have evidence that I can give major presentations successfully.' For example, be ready to be surprised by:

- the influence you can have on the attitude of key individuals,
- the willingness of people to listen to you,
- your effectiveness being greater than you had thought likely, and
- your understanding of the wide implications of a particular decision.

When you are surprised, celebrate that success and try to internalise it so that you are steadily adding to your repertoire of skills.

The importance of experimentation

Value-added is not about always doing the same thing. It is about varying new approaches and pushing the boundaries. It is about a continuous focus on experimentation, such as in the following example.

George, a CEO of a major engineering operation, talks of continuing to develop his value-added. He says:

'It is important to try to continually make space. I have developed space to move into more strategic roles. I have sometimes had to stand back from what I was naturally inclined to do to get people to come forward with their own plan. The key thing is then good questions and stretched targets linked with high expectations. It is important for the Chief Executive to set a framework but then not to try and run everything.

'The higher you go the more your value-added should become. Quite a lot of it is about positioning the business and pulling together some bigger themes. You have to handle the basics well. You have to be able to use the long screwdriver sometimes. But then you add value by asking questions and not taking things for granted.'

It is worth reflecting on:

- What experiments, in terms of how you add value, have worked best before?
- Are any of these experiments worth repeating?

- What else might you experiment with?

The value-added of enabling creativity in a team

Perhaps the most significant value-added that a leader can bring is about enabling creativity. Nicholas Ind and Cameron Watt, in their book *Inspiration: Capturing the Creative Potential of Your Organisation*, conclude that to enhance creativity you have to foster the right kind of leadership, recruit and develop the right kind of people and encourage the right culture: one based on empowerment, confidence and trust. They put a strong emphasis on listening and learning which depends on a unifying vision with individual members having an influence on its development. They see these as ingredients of a creative team:

- Team members should have high levels of professional competence to gain the respect of their colleagues, but they should not be egotistical.
- Diversity of background is valuable in bringing different perspectives to a problem, but there should also be a unifying ideology.
- There should be sufficient members of a team to tackle the problem at hand without creating a group that is too unwieldy and where decision making is difficult.
- There must be trust within the group and towards leadership but there should also be a challenge that stretches people's abilities.
- There must be clearly defined boundaries, but within those boundaries there should be freedom.

It is worth reflecting on:

- Which teams have you been part of that have been most creative?
- What features best helped that creativity?
- What might you do to replicate that creativity in teams which you lead or participate in?
- How important is creativity in the area you are currently working in?
- In what type of area do you want to bring creativity to your work?
- How relevant is bringing creativity in other areas of your life?

Bringing value-added from other spheres

Bringing value-added experience from other spheres can be very powerful. Sometimes we compartmentalise our lives between our work, family and community activities. We can gain much by thinking of the interaction between the different spheres we are involved in. We can encourage others to bring their value-added from an external sphere into their work situation.

For many years staff working in the Department for Education were not allowed to be school governors because of a potential 'conflict of interest'. In the early 1990s this policy was changed on the basis that the benefits to be gained by enabling members of the Department to be governors far outweighed any potential risks about conflict of interest. If an individual had the experience of being a governor in a school or college that gave them a whole new perspective which would enable them to do their job in the Department that much more effectively. In recent years there has been strong encouragement within the Department for individuals to take on this form of responsibility and thereby gain considerably in experience and understanding.

It is worth asking ourselves where do we add particular value in our lives outside our work? Are some of those skills transferable? For example:

- If we take a leadership role on a school governing body, in a club or society, at a church or mosque, can we use those skills effectively in other spheres?
- Are we more effective listeners outside the workplace because we are pacing our lives differently? Can we transfer any of those listening skills into the work situation?

An alternative way of looking at this is to consider the skills you need to grow in a work situation and whether what you do outside the office can help you grow those skills. Some examples I have come across recently are these.

William needed to develop his project management skills in the work situation. He was skilled in making wooden tables and thought hard about the processes he went through in order to design and build the tables. He reflected on how those stages which are highly relevant for carpentry could be transferred into a work situation.

Barbara wanted to develop her skills in risk management and took up rock climbing as a hobby. Doing this rigorous exercise effectively depended on a careful step-by-step approach to managing risk. With this experience she felt much more confident in thinking through next steps on risk management in a work situation.

Javed knew he would be called upon to chair more meetings in his work situation. He volunteered to chair an important community group at his local Sikh temple which was going to give him invaluable experience in chairing meetings.

Colin was conscious that he would have to give more presentations in his work. He offered to lead some seminars at his local church which gave him invaluable experience and strengthened his confidence considerably.

Adding value through the power of conversation

A crucial way in which we add value is how we use the power of conversation. Using conversation in the right way means the efficient use of time in reaching conclusions and in engendering commitment. In my book *Conversation Matters: How to Engage Effectively with One Another* I suggest that the best of conversations engage, discern and stretch.

Effective engagement is about:

- building trust,
- clear confidentiality rules,
- engendering openness,
- providing stillness amidst conversation to give people an opportunity to reflect,
- finding space to talk face-to-face,
- using humour to see the funny side of situations, and
- making conversation a shared journey of discovery.

Discernment is about:

- clarity of purpose in entering a conversation,
- questions that open up issues rather than close them down,
- curiosity, aiming to understand why a particular issue is important to somebody,
- experimentation so that we are not always predictable creatures of habit,
- taking risks in terms of sharing, and
- brevity in drawing out clear points and conclusions.

Stretching is about conversations that:

- are dynamic – you cannot predict the end of a conversation at its start,
- include a healthy level of debate working through difficult issues,

- transcend boundaries, deliberately entering conversations with people of different ages, cultures, personal circumstances and faiths,
- variable in speed with a sensitivity to when to move on to a new topic or have another round of coffee,
- provide challenge so that conversations are not too inward-looking or comfortable,
- bring freshness and express things in different ways,
- include a compelling modesty with a strong focus on listening, and are
- a means to an end so that conversations are not just enjoyable in themselves but lead to a richness of conclusions and a building of relationships.

Each person can add value through the power of conversation. Being sensitive to how we use the opportunity of conversation and varying our style and approach can ensure a wonderful adaptability in the way we add value.

Importance of feedback to refine value-added

One of the most powerful ways of refining your value-added is to gain an accurate understanding of how people perceive your skills and your contribution. There are various 360° feedback written tools available: some organisations have their standard 360° feedback tools on their internal intranet system. More powerful is when the feedback is done orally by an experienced coach who can probe the responses of individuals when they are collecting the feedback. Key steps are to ask an individual's colleagues about that person, covering things like:

- where they add value most effectively,
- where they least add value,
- how they could add value most effectively in the future, and
- what the biggest impact is that the individual could have on other people's development and performance.

Sometimes the feedback suggests the need for changes that are not all that time consuming. Often the way forward is through improving the quality of the interaction rather than its quantity. Conclusions are often such things as these:

- 'If he gave me his sole undivided attention when he spoke to me that would have such a powerful impact.'

- 'If I knew that she was listening and had heard what I said that would help greatly.'
- 'The occasional specific word of thanks would demonstrate she had noticed.'
- 'I do not want general comments about the fact I am doing well, I want focused, constructive comments that reinforce my learning so that I can continually improve my impact.'

Feedback is the best gift you can give a colleague. One of the most influential lessons to me was when one of my direct reports was very explicit, saying to me:

- 'You get too involved in the detail, that specificity is for me to do;
- the value-added you can bring most is through your influence with Ministers and across Government Departments;
- I want your focused attention on particular issues when you are not distracted and I can use you as a sounding-board on difficult issues;
- keep pushing me to look ahead and to be clear about the implications of what we are doing.'

Value-added as a mentor

Being a mentor can be a very valuable experience for both the mentor and for the mentee. Mentoring is a relationship between two individuals where the mentor draws on their experience to help the mentee work through new responsibilities and demanding situations. The mentor is a sounding board and sometimes a guide. The mentor does not impose their views on the mentee but may help them think through different options. The benefits for you as the mentor can include:

- clarifying your own ideas and approaches,
- learning from how the mentee approaches an issue,
- developing your listening skills so you are helping someone to think through issues without imposing your view on them,
- building a wider perspective,
- the joy of seeing someone grow and develop, and
- providing a valuable addition for your CV.

The benefits for the mentee can include:

- helping to clarify specific issues,
- access to new networks,

- a greater confidence in working with senior people,
- a greater ability to work through difficult issues,
- the pleasure of seeing how a more senior person would handle demanding situations,
- the sense of problems becoming less because they have been shared, and
- the opportunity to share successes.

Finding time to mentor is a serious commitment. Slotting it in over breakfast, a sandwich lunch or an early evening drink can provide a context that is relaxing as well as purposeful. Mentoring is always going to be worth the time. For example, mentoring a young person in the same organisation or in a different organisation will always give you insights about how the next generation is viewing particular issues. That perception will never be wasted.

The ultimate value-added: to work your way out of a job

We often think that the person who adds best value is the one who is most indispensable. The greatest value-added may be to work your way out of a job. For example:

- The football trainer adds value before the big match but has no part to play when the match is played.
- The senior manager has added value to the negotiating team prior to key discussions but will always leave the negotiating team to do their job without breathing over their shoulders.
- The main breadwinner in a family adds value by bringing in the income but does not dominate decisions on how the resources are spent.
- The parents will be adding value for their teenagers in terms of material and emotional support in the most unobtrusive of ways.

The most influential person will often not be the loudest but the person who adds wise points at key moments that influence the direction of travel.

The best of leaders will be working themselves out of a job because:

- the task has been completed,

- the team have developed their own skills in a way in which the leadership becomes unnecessary, or
- the introduction of new technology or partnerships has meant that the role is no longer necessary.

A valuable question to ask yourself when starting any job is 'How can I so use my influence in this role to make the job unnecessary in the future through the people I develop and the systems I put in place?' Sometimes we cling on to our roles rather than celebrating our part in making them unnecessary.

It is worth reflecting on:

- Is there a natural end point for my contribution?
- How well am I doing developing my potential successes?
- How would I feel if I worked myself out of this current role?

Finding your way through transitions

Because of the changing nature of employment many more of us are going through frequent transitions. These are moments when we can re-evaluate our value-added: they can be painful times, but also creative times. When one worthwhile stream of work comes to an end, being able to think openly about new opportunities is a gift. There is always a danger that we blinker ourselves by what we have done before or else colour the whole future with a pessimistic outlook.

After ten years as a board member in Government Departments it was time for me to move on. It was a heart-searching time of transition. My best adviser was my then 21-year-old son who said 'Pretend you are 21 again, what would you really like to do?' The value-added I most enjoyed bringing was in one-to-one conversations, trying to help people make sense of individual situations and move on in a positive way. Through the encouragement of my son and support from others I became increasingly clear that where I could add most value in the future was through coaching work. It had always been a pleasure and now it became a passion. The transition was not straightforward as I had explored a number of possibilities before being entirely sure that coaching was the way for me to add value in the future.

William Bridges wrote a particularly influential book called *Transitions:*

Making Sense of Life's Changes. He includes a transition checklist:

- Take your time: the outer forms of our lives can change in an instant, but the inner reorientation that brings us back into a vital relation to people and activity takes time.
- Arrange temporary structures: don't rush into a full and final solution.
- Don't act for the sake of action: avoid the temptation to 'do something – anything'.
- Recognise why you are uncomfortable: understanding transition process means expecting times of anxiety and expecting old fears to be re-awakened.
- Take care of yourself in little ways: for example, eat bananas if they are special for you.
- Explore the other side of change: try to see the benefits that will undercut your anger at whoever forced the change on you or you may realise that the old situation wasn't all that you thought it was.
- Get someone to talk to: but be aware of a listener who 'knows exactly what you want to do'.
- Find out what is waiting in the wings of your life: clear the ground for new growth. What new growth is ready to germinate in this season of your life?
- Use the transition as the impetus to a new kind of learning: be ready to acquire new understandings and new skills.
- Recognise that transition has a characteristic shape: things end, there is a time of fertile emptiness and then things begin anew.

Bringing together your strands of value-added

Suma Chakrabarti has had a huge impact in ensuring the Department for International Development has a much greater influence within government. He describes his value-added as changing over time. When he first arrived at the Department his value-added was based on his links elsewhere in Whitehall. He had previously had three major roles in Central Departments and knew all the key people well.

As time went on his main value-added was being more of a mentor. He took great pride in key staff whom he had grown and developed. Sometimes his mentoring was systematic; on other occasions it was ad hoc, arising out of particular situations. He thoroughly enjoyed helping people think through issues and enabling them to reach their own conclusions.

Suma was very clear that when he visited his staff in a third world country he was not there to give them grand messages. He wanted to work with them on live projects. It was through brainstorming with them on local strategic issues that he kept fresh in terms of his perception of development issues. It was a delight to him to be able to bring his experience to bear in a specific context.

In his first year as Permanent Secretary his focus was on leading the change agenda to ensure that the Department was modernised and alert. With his colleagues outside the Department his role with peers on cross-departmental groups was to challenge when people were too comfortable. This did not always make him popular but he saw it as important to bring a distinctive contribution that challenged the status quo.

Suma felt that where he added value most was giving people courage. People often assume that they cannot make change happen effectively. 'Be courageous and just do it' was his message. The results of Suma's courage are clear in the Department's success through reinforcing of the messages about combating poverty through the 'Make Poverty History' campaign, and decisions following the G8 July 2005 Conference in Edinburgh leading to significant increases in aid for Africa.

Can I encourage you to self-assess how you are going to add value in the future? Push yourself to add value in different ways:

- Build very clearly on your strengths.
- Experiment with adding value in different ways.
- Draw from previous experience and current experience outside the workplace continually.
- Be ready to sharpen particular skills, e.g. chairing meetings or giving presentations.
- Be clear what sort of value-added is most needed by those you work with.
- Be courageous and do things in ways that develop and reinforce the courage in others.

Can I encourage you to note down on a piece of paper how you have added value most in the last week? Answer questions like these:

- In which situations have I made the biggest difference?
- Which people have I influenced the most?
- Which people have I encouraged the most?
- Do I think anybody will have remembered the contribution that I made this last week?

A week later ask yourself the same questions, and then ask yourself:

- In what ways do I particularly want to add value next week?
- How am I going to experiment in the way I add value next week?
- What legacy do I want to leave behind next week?
- What are the words I want others to use in a week's time to describe the type of contribution I have made?

As you reflect on this chapter, the key questions you might ask yourself are:

- Have I developed the ways in which I am adding value in a clear way?
- Where can I add value more over the next six months?
- In what ways am I now going to experiment?
- How am I going to ensure that I am courageous?

Chapter 5:

Vitality

You can fool some of the people all the time and all of the people some of the time; but you can't fool all the people all of the time.
Abraham Lincoln

Our vitality levels go up and down often in unpredictable ways. The individual who can harness their energy in the most effective way is the person most likely to stay the course when others fall by the wayside. Our vitality levels can be completely unpredictable and depend on external circumstances. A key question is how best do we understand and harness our sources of vitality. The definition of vitality used in this book is 'energy which enables you to maintain a positive outlook across the different spheres of your life'.

This chapter deliberately does not start with work/life balance. So much has been said and written on this subject. The heart of addressing the vitality issue is to look at the causes of our levels of energy and how best we can nurture our sources of energy. Key questions are:

- What makes us want to go to work in the morning?
- What energises us at work?
- What keeps us going on a busy day?
- When we are tired and exhausted, what is it about our work which makes us still view it positively?

The themes addressed in this chapter cover:

- Sources of vitality.
- Growing vitality.

- Leading with energy and transmitting energy.
- Maintaining vitality.
- Linking vitality and personal happiness.

Sources of vitality at work

The same individual can be energised in one role, but feel exhausted working a limited number of hours in another role because they are bored, with a lack of stimulation. Some people may be working long hours, but because of the intrinsic job interest and stimulation the time flies by. They are neither bored nor disengaged: they arrive at the end of the day tired but fulfilled.

How can we best ensure that we use our own energy levels in the most effective way at work? It helps if we can assess these questions:

- When in the day are we at our most creative?
- What sort of rhythm of work best energises us? We may not often be in control of this but if a variety of work is important to us, can we try and arrange some variety within our working day?
- What is the best use of gaps during the working day? Is there an opportunity for a quick five-minute walk?
- How do we use the lunch 'break'? What is the best way of using it in terms of recharging our batteries?
- What do we do if our energy begins to flag? How can we best correct for that?
- Do we receive advance warning if we are beginning to be tired? Are we self-aware about how this affects our judgement?

It can be worthwhile to be very explicit in planning your diary, taking into account when your energy levels are likely to be at their highest so that the most demanding tasks can be put into that space. Keeping the more routine tasks for those times of day when energy levels are low can provide a sense of fulfilment, even when these tasks are not intrinsically rewarding.

For some people routine is crucial for ensuring energy levels are high: for others variety is crucial. If your place of work changes, you may need to learn a whole new discipline about keeping up energy levels. Claire has the privilege of working in Central London: she walks from Waterloo Station to Piccadilly each morning over Hungerford Bridge and across Trafalgar Square. A brief walk into St. James's Park or Green Park at lunchtime provides the stimulus she often needs to think in a fresh way.

Occasionally she works at home, when it is even more important to have periods of enforced exercise. If she did not make herself have a burst of fresh air her productivity would drop dramatically.

Helping other people feel energised

We have a responsibility to ourselves in terms of keeping up our energy levels. But we also have a responsibility to our colleagues and our staff in terms of whether we energise or depress them. The quality of interaction between us and our colleagues will either dampen their enthusiasm or recharge their energy levels. We should never underestimate the impact we have on our colleagues in any conversation.

With our own staff we have a particular responsibility: we set a tone in terms of encouraging commitment. The more we help people identify their most effective value-added the more their energy levels will be naturally high.

Key issues for us as managers are:

- Do we understand what energises individual members of staff?
- Do we take account of this understanding in the requests we make of staff?
- Do we have open feedback arrangements, whereby there is a clear understanding of the impact there is from one person on another in terms of energy levels?
- Do we see changes over time in the energy levels of different members of our staff and do we understand why that is happening?
- Do we use acts of recognition or small celebrations in a way which responds to the commitment of individual members of staff?
- Do we have a clear plan for the future in terms of maintaining and enhancing the energy levels of our staff?

A careful eye on encouraging vitality among staff and enabling that vitality to flower is perhaps the greatest gift we can bring as a leader. Leaders who inspire their staff draw out those reserves of energy which may have been long hidden.

Importance of experimentation

There has been a growing trend to have awaydays or training days to encourage groups of staff to take a fresh look at important issues. Such awaydays, with a varied approach and possibly a location away from the main office, often prove effective in encouraging people to 'think out of the box' and address issues with new energy.

Experimentation can bring a freshness essential for vitality. In their book *How to Start a Creative Revolution at Work*, the writers from the creative consultancy ?What If! focus on the importance of freshness. They say that the raw material for creativity is constantly topped up by a deep, almost childlike curiosity about the world. Whether by design or instinct (or a bit of both) the most creative people and organisations ensure a very varied diet. Freshness can be both a personal and a corporate behaviour. They see freshness as:

- Re-expression: finding an alternative way of describing or experiencing the issue or problem.
- Related worlds: looking at other areas where a similar issue or benefit can be seen.
- Revolution: identifying and then challenging the rules and assumptions we are using.
- Random links: making connections and links between the issue and random items found in the world.

For example, they look at different ways of re-expression:

- re-expression with alternative words,
- re-expression using different senses, and
- re-expression from someone else's perspective.

Freshness is so important to our wellbeing, be it fresh air, fresh food or fresh water alongside fresh ideas and fresh pathways. Freshness is both about how we approach our work and about the interplay between the range of activities we are involved in. But sometimes vitality comes through repeated activities which we particularly enjoy. George, the CEO of a major engineering concern, says that key aspects of vitality for him are playing golf and being engrossed with his family. These are part of his weekly pattern which are very important to his wellbeing. He says that he never talks to his wife about the details of the job. When he plays golf with friends he doesn't talk about his work. For him being with his family or playing golf is an escape from work where he can completely relax. As a CEO, he has never worked through a weekend. He admits to sometimes doing some emails, but the weekend is his opportunity to relax.

For others vitality comes through doing something completely different. For a former colleague, now very senior within the Civil Service, relaxation also came at weekends – through getting cheap flights to very different destinations. Exploring a range of European cities was the stimulus he wanted to enable him to forget the day-to-day tasks, be intellectually and aesthetically stimulated and see the world in a much wider perspective.

To what extent does your vitality come from:

- Doing what you enjoy and are good at?
- Absorbing yourself in new experiences?

What new experiences would help give you new vitality? Could they be things like:

- Walking in places that you have never walked before?
- Visiting cities you have never been to before?
- Listening to music that is new to you?
- Meeting very different people?
- Being immersed in the work of a particular charity?

One friend who is the Chief Executive of a Government Agency tells of the importance for him of working in the winter at an overnight shelter for homeless people. In this role he is not the chief executive, he is someone making the tea, and talking with depressed and cold homeless people. My friend feels compassionate about the plight of these people: at the same time this labour of love puts his work into perspective and helps give him energy in order to do his job in a way that will bring equity and fairness to a significant number of people.

Be ready to be surprised by what gives you vitality. Be open-minded about whether you will enjoy a film that your partner or daughter wants you to see. When you escort a child to participate in a sporting event, be ready to be surprised by your own reaction when boredom turns into entertainment as you appreciate the enthusiasm and commitment that the youngsters are putting into the sport.

What are our sources of vitality in other spheres of life?

Asking ourselves about our sources of vitality in different areas of our life can provide a creative way of looking at the balance of our life activities.

What are the sources of energy in your different spheres of life? They might be:

- your family,
- your community,
- your belief world,
- physical recreation,
- wider intellectual interests,
- the arts and music ...

In each of these spheres there is likely to be something that enthuses you. Part of the test of enthusing is whether something engages your full attention and whether you feel better or worse as a result of spending time on that particular activity. For example:

- Your children will be a source of fresh enthusiasm and new life (well, most of the time).
- There may be a particular satisfaction in sharing in local community activities such as the drama group, the Rotary Club or voluntary activities like working with the elderly.
- Your belief world may well be an important source of calmness and purpose.
- Physical recreation may well be both painful and exhilarating in recharging your batteries.
- It may be music or the theatre that is best able to 'calm your fears' and 'nurture your passions'.

Sometimes we can see our enjoyment of sport and work on a collision course; if we are working hard and then playing cricket on Saturday the family time is squeezed. Difficult choices inevitably have to be made. The choices will not necessarily be equal in their significance: family commitments are not optional, be they in relation to children, parents, spouse or partner. There will be choices about how these family commitments are fulfilled, but not an option about whether they are fulfilled. The key issue is what activities outside family and work responsibilities are most precious in:

- recharging your batteries,
- giving you an equitable perspective on life,
- providing humour and lightness, and
- enabling you to do your work even better because you are that much more fulfilled in your life outside work.

Taking forward the vitality theme does mean:

- Identifying what activities outside work give you most energy
- How can you grow those areas of vitality?
- What is the learning from those areas of vitality you can transfer into your work context?

The relationship between comfort zone and vitality

Listening to your favourite music, supporting your favourite football team or cooking your favourite food provides a routine which gives you the calmness essential to nurture energy within. Routine is crucial to give you a rhythm of life without which your vitality cannot be refreshed, but going outside that comfort zone is just as important in terms of growing those sources of vitality.

- If walking four miles makes you feel energised, why not five or six?
- If going to the gym twice a week seems to make a big difference, why not three times a week?
- If listening to Beethoven's String Quartets gives you the stimulus you need, why not try some modern string quartet music?

Interconnecting sources of vitality

It is worth reflecting on how different individuals interconnect different sources of energy. When in conversation with colleagues, reflect on what gives them vitality: what is the balance between their different activities? An example is Rosemary, a senior executive in a national private-sector organisation. She puts a strong focus on personal planning. If she did not do so she would run herself into the ground. Her vitality comes from friends and sport. Vitality with friends is crucial and she still sees some friends from school on a regular basis; she is meticulous about keeping in touch with them. At the last New Year she identified eleven friends whom she and her husband wanted to meet in the first three months of the year, and they are planning holidays around their American and German friends. Family is equally important to Rosemary: she sees her German family four times a year, which is very important to her. She gets energy from helping people. Recently a good friend had breast cancer: she received a great deal of energy from being with her friend, encouraging and helping her.

Rosemary thoroughly enjoys her work but it is the sources of vitality outside the office that are crucial in giving her fulfilment. Sport is one: as a youngster she did well at both education and sport. Part of her upbringing was doing her academic work first before she could do the sport. Now she strives to do both. She goes to the gym on Tuesdays, plays tennis on Wednesday, goes to the gym again on Saturdays and plays golf or tennis on Sundays. She is conscious that she needs to eat in a healthy way: the better she eats the healthier she feels.

For Rosemary, vitality at home comes through carefully planning events and enjoying the close company of friends and family. Vitality at work is very different. It comes through:

- interaction with colleagues and clients,
- positive reinforcement from the encouragement of colleagues,
- involvement in high-profile issues that are exhausting but give her a great buzz, and
- the pleasure of being with a range of different people in a work context.

Recognising that vitality levels vary considerably

We have to a large extent to live within the capacities that we have been given. Sometimes we can train ourselves in different ways through time management and through the way we organise our activities and allow ourselves to be encouraged by others. Observing others can help us use our energies in the most constructive way. I encourage the people I work with to observe others continuously and to decide what approaches they can take on themselves.

John Dunford, the General Secretary of the Association of School and College Leaders, admits that he is very fortunate. He does not require much sleep, and is happy to spend a lot of time working. He has had leadership positions for over thirty years. His safety valve is early in the morning: if something needs to be done he will get up at 5 a.m. and do it. The danger is thinking that if something needs to be done he should do it. He says that he is now getting much better at delegating. He has now adjusted to taking a full three-week holiday in the summer and completely relaxing in this period.

John admits to doing work at the weekend but he ensures it is at a time which is not disruptive to his family. He says he often works between 5 a.m. and 9 a.m. on Saturday and Sunday mornings, using this period to get major pieces of work done. The rest of the weekend is free to spend with his family, and this recently included putting up shelves in his daughter's flat. Finding space to relax when he is in London during the week is more difficult. He always walks from location to location in London in order to get physical exercise and also have an essential moment to reflect between meetings.

John is unusual in needing relatively little sleep, but he does provide an example of how, if work demands are high, part of the answer is to box the time for work in a focused way so that it has minimum disruption on family and friends.

Acknowledging that vitality can come from being driven

We have differing attitudes to the work. For some work is hard labour. For others there is a driven-ness about our attitude to work that does have positive benefits.

For example, Andrew Higginson, the Finance and Strategy Director for Tesco, talks of the importance of being honest with yourself. Andrew's view is that you must recognise how driven you are. Andrew is in his late forties and enjoys his job enormously. He acknowledges that perhaps he has been a bit selfish with his time but he does not completely regret that as he gets enormous satisfaction out of his work. The stimulus of his work keeps reinforcing his energy. Even when his work is very busy he is able to find moments when he can relax at work because he enjoys his work so much.

When he is not working, Andrew's time with his family and friends is important. Running is a source of energy. Flicking through TV channels is his indulgence. Andrew's contrasting world is education where he is chair of a secondary school governing body. Andrew is an utterly delightful modest leader. Part of his success is understanding the ways in which he is driven and what gives him energy both at work and in his personal life.

It may be worth reflecting on:

- What drives us to succeed?
- Do we channel that drive effectively?
- How do we best balance that drive with other interests and responsibilities?

Doing something completely different

If your passion is to do something very different outside your work you can take heart from examples of senior leaders who obtain their vitality both from doing their job well and from doing something completely different. Ken Boston, the Australian Chief Executive of the U.K. Qualifications and Curriculum Authority, gets his vitality at work through enabling his direct reports to do their jobs effectively. He says 'The virtue of my age is that I can genuinely mentor my direct reports. It is great to bring them on and give them oxygen.' He gets a lot of satisfaction from writing and giving speeches and seeing his ideas coming to fruition, 'when I see the ground move'.

Outside his work his energy comes from his family, who have come from Australia to live with him in London. He enjoys long walks at weekends and going to the theatre. He works very hard in the day but aims to be home at 7 p.m. with just a few briefing notes for the following day to read late in the evening. His greatest relaxation is reading, and he insists on spending an hour a day reading books not connected with education or training, consuming books voraciously. Recent reads have been Lord Norwich's *History of Venice*, Max Hastings' *Armageddon* and some recently written history books about the Second World War. Special relaxation comes from reading the poetry of Yeats and Graves. At the weekend he will spend much more than an hour a day reading. Ken Boston's message on vitality is:

- Limit the amount of work time: as you progress in a career do not allow yourself to do an excessive number of hours.
- Stay in charge of your time and control your diary.
- Don't have an 'open door' policy all the time but have focused occasions when you are available.
- Regularly take stock about how you are spending your time: only do what no one else can do.
- When you get snowed under it is a warning sign that you need to review the pattern of how you are spending your time.

Is there any aspect of Ken Boston's experience that might be especially relevant for you in terms of:

- Staying in control of your time and diary?
- The timing of your availability to others?
- Your reaction when you feel snowed under?

Vitality and time management

The effective use of time is an important part of how we nurture our vitality. Jean, the managing director of a regional organisation, is intrigued by where people get their energy from and how they use their time. She has a huge amount of it: she doesn't know where it comes from but thinks it results from a positive outlook and personal determination. She admits to having a work/life balance that could be improved. She starts work between 7 a.m. and 7.30 a.m. and is at her most alert between then and 10 a.m., with this time being used for her own personal work. She will then have a busy day of meetings. Ideally she goes home at 5 p.m. and then has a burst of work at home between 6 p.m. and 8 p.m.

Jean is reasonably content with this pattern as she believes that she is able to have a significant influence for good in her job. Key sources of energy for her are her close friends and half-an-hour of meditation each morning which helps clear her mind for the day.

Her meditation is about going through an affirming process envisaging working to the best of her ability with positive relationships with her colleagues. Jean sees herself as a spiritual but not a religious person. A key driver for her is behaving to others as she would want them to behave to her. She feels much 'blessed' in her life and work. This gives her a richness of vitality which helps her have a positive outlook and keeps her level of vitality high.

Vitality and positive thinking

It is perhaps too trite to say 'always try to think positively'. But we all know that it makes such a difference. When we describe a bottle as half-full rather than half-empty we are conditioning ourselves to be clear that we are halfway to success rather than nowhere near success. The interaction between viewing where we are as good progress rather than poor performance on our energy levels is all too apparent. This is not about deluding ourselves, but it is about being clear on progress made. It is about setting milestones that are attainable so that we keep up our energy levels.

In any demanding situation it is worth reflecting on:

- what is going really well,
- what progress we have been making,

- what opportunities there are to move the issue on, and
- how we could grow through this experience.

For me, one of the small joys in life is talking to taxi drivers. I recently had two very different conversations. Both drivers were in their mid fifties. The first one was bemoaning his lot: the car was squeaking, the customers were difficult, the job was tiring. He couldn't wait until he could retire from driving a taxi. The next taxi driver had bought a house in Norfolk and lived there from Friday afternoon till Monday morning. He came back into London to drive his taxi from Monday to Friday lunchtime. He enjoyed the variety, the people and the conversations. Taxi driving was fun. There were sometimes problems but he had no wish to retire. This comparison is of two people doing the same job with similar incomes with completely different attitudes of mind. It is reflecting on these sharp contrasts that enable us to be clearer about the positive dimensions of the situations in which we find ourselves.

What is your oxygen mask?

A couple of years ago when travelling with my family from San Francisco to London two of our youngsters were ill and had to have oxygen masks. This was in one sense a curious novelty and in another a great relief. Using the oxygen mask is a necessary part of survival. If we use the oxygen mask too often we become over-dependent upon it. But knowing it is there and available is a great reassurance. It is well worth being clear what our oxygen masks are. When we are busy at work it might be:

- the brief walk at lunchtime,
- a photograph of the sea or the family on the desk,
- the brief telephone call with our spouse or partner,
- the exchange of smiles with a great colleague, or
- reflecting briefly on a job well done.

Knowing what your oxygen mask is and using it is a sign of strength, not weakness. It is worth considering:

- What is your oxygen mask?
- When has it been most useful?
- How readily do you use it?
- How do you ensure that you do not become too dependent on it?

Using weekends and holidays effectively

If the weekends are just for collapsing and sleeping there may be something wrong. For many of us weekends are about family or community life. Lively youngsters or aging parents will engage much of our time and emotional energy. Weekends that nurture our vitality are often connected with:

- Enjoying routine activities: cutting the grass can be so therapeutic
- Giving ourselves some moments of peace and quiet
- Operating at a different speed from when we are at work – maybe quicker when we push the pedals on our bicycle or slower as we do the ironing
- Doing something completely different which makes us smile.

We give up holidays at our peril. When I was young my father had just two weeks of holiday a year. He worked a five-and-a-half-day week, so holidays were precious. He took the two weeks together in one block, visiting the same hotel in Bournemouth over a number of years. His source of relaxation was to be walking by the sea. As a family, holidays have been very special. Our children are now in their twenties but will still join us on holiday for a week each summer. When I work with senior managers I encourage them:

- Never to begrudge money spent on holidays.
- To vary the pattern and do different things.
- To enjoy the simple as well as the extravagant: taking the family to a youth hostel can be just as enjoyable as a luxury hotel.

Capturing the memories can be so important. It isn't just taking the photographs, it is displaying them in some way. In our hallway we have a collage of photographs which constantly remind us of time spent as a family. Keeping talking about enjoyable holidays can be a constant source of renewed vitality.

Relevance of spirituality

For many people their religious faith is crucial in providing clarity about their purpose in life and a sense of fulfilment and calmness. Within the Christian tradition there are dominant themes which provide an important focus on the renewal of energy. These include:

- new birth: old ways can change and there can be new horizons,
- conversion: it is possible to turn around and move from a sense of emptiness to fullness,
- forgiveness: it is possible to be released from the burden of guilt and move into a new joy, and
- resurrection: whatever has gone wrong it is possible to be renewed and reinvigorated.

These themes are an important source of energy for those of Christian faith. Christians also see God as present in the world through his Spirit who helps the believer to bring a positive approach whatever the circumstances.

A religious background can on occasion be a negative as well as a positive influence. Sometimes it can mean that an individual is driven in a way that is blinkered. If the Protestant work ethic drives someone to focus so hard at work that they have a limited involvement in wider interests, their energy for making a difference can run low. Those who share the same faith have a duty to ensure that those in the same community of faith do not become so blinkered that they lose the width of interests and vitality necessary to keep the community alive.

Religious faith is a profound source of vitality for leaders coming from the Christian, Jewish, Muslim, Hindu and Sikh traditions. There is now a much wider interest in spiritual intelligence as a source of vitality. Danah Zohar and Ian Marshall have described spiritual intelligence as the soul's intelligence – the intelligence with which we heal ourselves and with which we make ourselves whole. They see as indicators of a highly developed spiritual intelligence the capacity to be flexible, a high degree of self-awareness, a capacity to face and transcend pain, the quality of being inspired by vision and values, a marked tendency to ask fundamental questions and possessing a facility for working against convention. They see spiritual intelligence in leaders as helping them to be creative, to deal with the unexpected, to see unity behind difference, to reach more fully the people we have the potential to be and to wrestle with the problems of good and evil.

One of the benefits of a greater recognition of the value of diversity in our world today is the acceptance that the religious traditions bring particular insights which include developing in individuals a strong sense of service, generosity and self-sacrifice. Vitality comes from giving as much as receiving.

The insight from religious traditions that vitality comes from giving is highly relevant to the way leaders and organisations enable people to give. The organisation that sponsors a charity or enables people to support their own charities through topping up their giving can release new vitality in their staff which is to the benefit of both the individual and the organisation.

Keeping the distance between different activities

Keeping clear boundaries between different activities can be an important way of ensuring strong energy levels. Part of the picture is the energy we draw from work, but an essential element is the distance that we can put between work and other activities.

As an example, David Adleman, a principal of a sixth form college, draws significant energy at work from the pleasure of managing the organisation. He likes the transparency of watching the organisation grow and develop and enjoys the problem solving of individual challenges relishing their variety. Being courteous to a complaining parent is just as important as being firm with the building contractor.

David deliberately lives a long way from where he works. Leisure for him is about taking off his uniform and being a different person. As he drives over the South Downs in Sussex each evening he metaphorically 'takes his suit off'. When he is at home he can be more himself. It is always important to him to be gracious and welcoming: vitality comes from his bonds with good friends where there is a strong sense of justice and improving society.

Those who work in a big city like London often have the disadvantage of the commuting journey but the advantage of that separation between home and work. Someone can be very senior in the City and completely anonymous in Dorking. Allowing that separation between home and work and using it as a benefit requires a particular attitude of mind. The commuter can be dragged down by the tedium of rail travel or enervated by that natural divide between work and home, using the safety valve of the train journey to go through the in-tray, read a novel or listen to music on the iPod.

Putting distance between work and home is more difficult with greater opportunity to work partly from home. It depends on having as clear boundaries as possible about where and when one works in the home. It may be worth reflecting on:

- Am I clear when I am working and when I am not working?

- Should I be clearer about the boundaries?
- What is the best way of ensuring the necessary separation?

Passion as part of vitality

Passion to make a difference is a central part of vitality. Nick Bollettieri has an outstanding record as a tennis coach with Agassi, Seles and the Williams sisters. When asked what these star players shared he said:

> 'Passion. Whether it is in business or life, a champion has to have it. There are people that bounce along in life, and people that bounce but in the wrong direction, and then there are those that are consumed by their passion. It even burns when they go to sleep, during their sleep, and when they wake in the morning, it's still burning. That's the attitude that divides my really gifted players from those that are just good.' (*The Times*, 25 June 2005)

If vitality results from what we are passionate about, a key test is understanding what in our work makes us passionate and how that passion can be focused to have the maximum benefit. It is worth reflecting sometimes, both in our work and in the other activities we are involved in, about:

- What aspects of the activity enthuse us?
- What are the outcomes we feel most passionate about?
- How can we harness that passion to the best possible effect?
- Is there a synergy between our personal passions and the most important outcomes for the organisation?
- Is our passion always helpful or is it sometimes blinkered?

In terms of his own vitality Nick Bollettieri is clear that 'there is no wealth that can buy the inner satisfaction of knowing you have had an impact on someone's life and helped create who they are.' Nick is in his mid-seventies. When pressed about whether the slippers and the pipe appealed he asserted,

> 'No, they never will. I'm working on a book about what you can do after 55 if you remain curious about your life. Think of Mother Theresa working night and day at 85, or Colonel Sanders starting up Kentucky Fried Chicken at 67. No one has the right to be tired. You can change direction, but you should never give up.'

Whatever age we are, it is worth reflecting on the vitality levels of those twenty years older:

- What is it that gives these people a sense of vitality and energy?
- What can I learn from the way they focus their efforts?
- Why is it that their enthusiasm is infectious?
- How can I embrace what I most appreciate about these people?

Leading with energy

Stanton Marris have produced an excellent set of booklets about the importance of leading with energy. They describe themselves as an 'organisational energy consultancy'. They have an outstanding track record of influencing focused change in national organisations. They say that leadership tasks critical to energising an organisation are:

- Creating energy: through being visible and sending the right signals, developing and supporting talent, creating alliances with key people.
- Providing purpose and direction: through lifting the sights, setting the tone, developing a cohesive and aligned top team, deciding the priorities and picking up early warning signals.

They set out two important touchstones for leaders transmitting their energy in demanding periods:

- How well do you lift the sights of the organisation? Leaders need to paint a picture of the future and talk about it at every opportunity, drawing a strong connection between the work people do and the positive impact it has.
- Setting the right tone is crucial. Under pressure it can feel natural to seek refuge in what is familiar and that is often facts, analysis and 'busyness'. Leaders may become invisible at critical times, tied up in meetings or paying more attention to the media than to their people. A crisis is an opportunity to send a signal; to demonstrate, in the glare of the spotlight, what is important.

Stanton Marris define organisational energy as 'the extent to which an organisation has mobilised the full available effort of its people in pursuit of its goal'. They see wasted organisational energy and vitality occurring in a number of different ways:

- In friction between parts.

- In activity that adds no value.
- In managing upwards, i.e. playing political games and watching your back.
- In failure to engage.
- In failure to inspire.

They see as sources of organisational energy:

- Connection: the importance that people have a line of sight between themselves, their work, their values and the purpose of the organisation.
- Content: is work organised in such a way that it is stimulating and provides a sense of achievement?
- Context: are the working practices and the work environment supportive and enabling? The emotional part is whether the individual feels the organisation supports them to do a good job and shows that it values them.
- Climate: how far does the typical 'local weather' of the organisation make people want to give their best and help them grow to their potential?

Stanton Marris have done some innovative work on 'Plotting the energy curve'. They see a three-wave approach of:

- discovering energy: exploring and measuring organisational energy,

Organisational energy curve

Discover wave	Focus wave	Release wave
• explore	• dialogue	• vision
• respect	• communication	• empowerment
• understand energy	• feedback	• share values

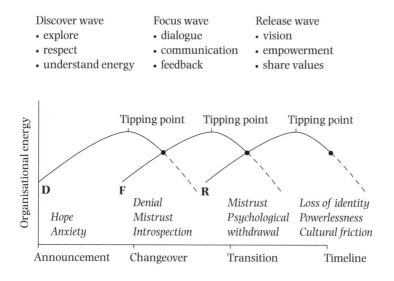

- focusing energy: shaping an agenda for action including capturing attention, and engaging the minds and emotions of others, and
- releasing energy: implementing processes, behaviours and actions that mobilise energy and keep you focused on the right things.

Their thesis is that people become energised when they have a sense of control over their own destiny and can contribute to improving business performance. If organisation energy is high, this can be an ideal time to tackle difficult issues. These ideas from Stanton Marris were written in terms of organisations. They are equally relevant to individuals using their own vitality to help raise levels of energy within organisations for which they have a leadership responsibility.

Transmitting energy

One of the most interesting parts of the Stanton Marris work is about transmitting energy. When you walk into a room there is often a sense of either energy or its absence. Too much energy of the wrong sort is a complete 'killer'. An individual bouncing around like a demented spaniel can sap energy rather than create it. Transmitting energy is about engagement, calmness and a clear sense of direction. It is worth reflecting on:

- In what situations have you felt your energy levels have risen?
- What have been the factors that have led to your feeling energised?
- How long did that energy last and how did you nurture it?
- What lessons are there for you in how you can convey energy to others?
- How much for you is it about drawing the energy out of people or giving something of your energy to them?

When under pressure?

It is one thing to be energised in activities when things are going well. It is another to have a strong sense of vitality when things are going less well. Those involved in sport are well aware of the impact that losing has on energy levels. Sometimes losing is a stimulus for new energy: at other times the energy is sapped and motivation is difficult. This is equally true in a work environment when we have to cope with the rollercoaster of success and failure. How do we keep the vitality levels in equilibrium?

Different techniques work for different people. Here are some possible pointers:

- Are you able to hold something in reserve? Even though you are busy, are you able to operate within your capacity so that you can put the accelerator down when needed? If the accelerator is always full down there is no new capacity for a crisis.
- Do you pace yourself effectively during the working day or week?
- Do you ensure there is some variety so that even when you are focusing on one crisis there is the opportunity to spend some time on activities which are completely different?
- Are you keeping up the rhythm of physical activity, however pressed you are in a work situation?
- What are the rewards you can give yourself that will help keep you going in very demanding situations? It may be something as trivial as a favourite bar of chocolate or a glass of whisky in the evening.
- Do you have a mutual understanding with close friends about how best you can be encouraged within that friendship when the going gets tough?

When you have been through a severe period of pressure it is worth reflecting on what has helped maintain effective vitality levels. What activities, colleagues or friendships have been most important? It is well worth being clear about what helped make the difference and then reflecting on how that experience can be embedded in your personal approach to future crises. Preparation this way can pay huge dividends.

Rhythm of vitality over a week

Are you at your best early in the morning or late in the evening? Are your most creative moments travelling in to work on the commuter train or in the car, talking with a friend over lunch or sitting with a glass of wine in an evening? Whatever your natural barometer, using your vitality to the full means:

- Working with your rhythms and using creative moments to the best possible effect.
- Varying your pattern so that you are stretching the way you develop your vitality and are not captive to one particular approach. The availability of email, whether through PCs, laptops and smaller devises like Blackberrys, provides another dimension of flexibility in terms of

using our vitality levels to the best possible effect. But these aids can sometimes feel like chains!

When writing this book I had bursts of activity at home preparing sections. These working times needed to be focused and not too long, with self-imposed targets about the amount I was going to write within a defined period. My vitality was best maintained moving in and out of writing, talking on the phone with colleagues, conversation with who-ever was at home and brisk walking. That combination was essential to me to keep up my energy and motivation. Writing is quite lonely and therefore needed to be interspersed with talking to real people.

There is a great joy about trying new ways of packaging your time to keep your energy levels high. Different means of recharging the batteries are invaluable. The rhythms that will work for us best will change depending on personal circumstance and preference. Experimentation is never wasted. Try thinking creatively while on the top of a double-decker bus, riding a bicycle or walking briskly: using a different rhythm might put your brain into a different gear.

The importance of special places, prose or poetry in nurturing vitality

All the religious traditions place an emphasis on special places for reflection. The sense of pilgrimage to a special place such as Iona, Holy Isle, Jerusalem or Mecca provides a rhythm and a purpose that brings a calmness and a refocusing of energy. The same principle is true for those without a religious perspective. It may be a special walk, a particular forest, some magnificent gardens or a peaceful view. Using special places in a regular and creative way can be powerful in calming fears, defining hopes and giving a peace of mind about next steps.

Where religious belief is important to you key passages can provide the rhythm that gives you space for reflection. They may be words directly from religious or liturgical texts or from meditations. It may be words that have been important to you or your family in earlier times that continue to have a strong resonance.

For others it might be the rhythm of some wonderful poetry which is special to you. Whatever the type of poetry that enables you to have space for reflection and put things in perspective, don't be embarrassed to read it regularly. Poetry may not be your poison, but maybe it is worth experimenting and giving yourself space to be absorbed in the rhythm of some good poems.

It is well worth reflecting on the special significance for you of:

- special places,
- significant pieces of prose or religious passages, or
- poetry which uplifts you,

and then building further on how you enjoy them.

Vitality and humour

Meetings with no humour can be so boring and sap the energy. Meetings where there is forced humour can be a groan. Discussions which include humour at the expense of individuals can be damaging and disheartening. But when a meeting includes laughter and a sense of fun the participants look up and are more positive.

Humour as a means of encouraging vitality is difficult to plan for but so powerful in its execution. Effective humour in meetings:

- lifts the spirits,
- provides a bonding between participants, and
- puts the issues of the day into a wider perspective.

Humour can come through:

- seeing the funny side of what has occurred,
- recounting an incident that had happened previously that is amusing and relevant,
- seeing the potential absurdities of different approaches,
- imagining how people would smile about particular solutions, or
- suggesting how an observer might view a particular situation in an amusing way.

One of the greatest skills in chairing a meeting is to be able to bring out humour in a way that enlivens a discussion without creating any sense of upset. It is a difficult pathway sometimes, but crucial to keeping vitality levels high. Developing effective learning in the use of humour depends on:

- a good self-understanding about what makes you laugh,
- an awareness about what types of humour can work best with others,

- a keen eye to see the funny side of different situations,
- allowing other people to use humour, and
- responding well when you are teased by others.

Vitality and fasting

The idea of fasting possibly seems dated and linked to religious practices of dubious relevance. But perhaps fasting needs to be rediscovered. The growth of modern technology has meant that our addictions have become more acute.

- We need to be up to speed all the time through using the mobile phone.
- We relish the instant communication of email.
- Some of us have a new toy like a Blackberry, which means we receive our emails wherever we are.
- In open plan offices, we are always accessible.

Fasting is sometimes about giving ourselves space when we turn the mobile phone off, do not turn the computer on and do not read our emails. Abstinence can provide a new sense of freshness when we spend some time not watching the television, not drinking alcohol and not consuming caffeine. Giving up chocolates or alcohol for Lent is not only physically and spiritually sensible, it may help put us back more in control of our emotions.

Fasting from favourite foods or indulgences can give us new vitality in enjoying different activities and also the rather special vitality of returning to that favoured indulgence after a period of abstinence. Many of us have spent a period fasting from carbohydrate food following some variant of the Atkins diet. We may debate the rights and wrongs but some of us have felt healthier as a result. It is worth thinking objectively about what types of abstinence might generate more vitality even though it might follow a period of craving the absent indulgence.

Importance of physical activity

Parks or riverside walks are relatively close to many offices in London. The deluge of people walking or jogging through the parks at lunchtime illustrates the increased emphasis on physical exercise. One former Foreign Secretary was frequently seen walking at lunchtime in St.

James's Park talking to his advisers. This break of routine was important for him in terms of his rhythm of the day.

An increasing number of people regularly use a gym; they talk of the sapping of their energy at work if they have not been on the rowing machine. The best relaxation for a colleague (aged 56) is playing cricket every summer weekend. He returns full of aches and pains, but is always invigorated.

Taking reasonably intense physical activity is not optional. The macho culture of saying there is no time for physical activity is short-sighted. It is not a matter of 'if' but of 'what type' of physical exercise. For my wife and I, a brisk walk every Saturday is important both so that we talk to each other and also so that we do get some physical exercise. I normally walk four miles a day, including walking to the local station and then from the station in London to my office in Pall Mall. On the occasions when I work at home my productivity goes down if I do not force myself to do some physical activity.

It is worth keeping asking these questions:

- What are the benefits for you in taking part in physical activity?
- What sort of physical activity do you most enjoy?
- What types of physical activity can you do more of?
- How can you experiment?
- How much time are you prepared to give to this type of activity?
- What are the resulting benefits of different forms of physical activity?

Wendy Grossman describes the top five excuses:

- I don't have the time.
- I don't know where to start.
- There's no gym near me.
- I don't have the money.
- I'm too old to start.

She writes about Josh Selzmann, a personal trainer. He says,

> 'You have to hard graft in the work context in a smart way. But when it comes to their bodies they don't do that. Unless you listen to what your body needs and do what it needs – exercise at the right time with the right fuel – you'll be working against yourself all the time. Many people go in and out of gyms and feel and look worse for it.' (*Daily Telegraph*, 16 June 2005)

His advice is:

- If you are starting an exercise programme do a lot less than you think. Start progressively.
- You are what you eat. Don't substitute more exercise for poor eating habits.
- You can get into the best shape of your life spending less than three hours a week total exercise time.
- If you lose weight quickly you'll gain it back quickly. Effective weight management is a lifestyle change.
- Emotional fitness is just as important as physical fitness. If you are not emotionally fit, you'll never really be able to get truly physically fit.
- Look at the glass as half-full. Look at everything as an opportunity to move forward to higher enlightenment.

The purpose of this section is not to encourage you to make physical fitness the be all and end all. It is to encourage you to ask the questions about where physical fitness sits and how you might take that forward in a stretching and realistic way.

Keeping vitality when work is boring and routine

Roland, aged 19, wanted to do a variety of jobs during a summer holiday before going to university. He enlisted with an agency and delivered post, packed boxes, filled envelopes and completed forms. One assignment involved inputting data: he got so bored that he began to add in amusing comments about the data. This was his means of keeping up his vitality; unfortunately this did not go down well with his boss and he was asked to leave. This was a good learning experience about how *not* to combat boredom when work is routine.

For all of us there are aspects of work which are boring but have to be done. Sometimes there is no escape from these boring tasks. When you are engaged in something boring it is worth reflecting on what will maintain your energy levels. Is it about:

- the time of day when the boring activities are done,
- the location where these activities are done so that the environment feels good,
- the people you are with and able to talk to during the periods of boredom,

- the rewards you promise yourself when the boring task is completed,
- persuading yourself about the value of the boring activity in the long run, or
- devising ways of reducing the boredom in these activities?

Boredom can also be an indicator that change is needed. If you are bored, others will be bored too. What can you do to change the environment? It may be bringing clarity about the purposes or the outcomes so that all those involved see the potential benefits of what is being done. If it is stuffing invitations into envelopes, then having a clear picture of the event to which people are being invited can give a valuable purpose to a boring task.

A crucial test for any leader is how can they help raise the spirits of those doing relatively boring work. It is about:

- Being clear on the overall context.
- Celebrating successes.
- Providing as much variety as possible within the constraints of the role.
- Being appreciative of specialist skills.
- Embedding learning opportunities that will enable somebody to move on to other less boring things.
- Recognising that for some people the routine and boring is really important in terms of providing a structure for life and taking them out of situations which they find saddening or frustrating.

Watch who saps your energy

Sometimes people and situations can drain us of energy. Often there is little we can do about it. But it is worth observing what is happening and why. Various friends have had situations where a difficult boss or a difficult member of staff has been a constant source of worry. Whenever they have tried to be rational there has been an irrational response. The result has been a sapping of their own confidence.

It is worth being very objective about why certain people sap your energy. If it means you need to spend less time in their company try to ensure that happens. If it means you have to say something directly to the individual to try and change the situation it is going to be well worth that investment and risk. If the solution that is necessary is for one of your staff to move on, because you sap each other's energy, then it is probably in both your interests for them to do so sooner rather than later.

One simple technique is to score your own vitality level after meetings with different individuals. That is often an effective measure of which working relationships are working well, which need some radical change.

The vitality from stopping doing things

Energy comes from trying new things or doing things we enjoy doing. Sometimes there is a release of energy by just stopping doing something:

- Are we over-loyal in our membership of a particular group which has ceased to energise us?
- Do we do certain things for the wrong reasons or because we have always done them?
- Is there a particular comfort about the routine of a particular activity which we ought to move on from?

There is a clear link to value-added and decisions about what things we should stop doing. It is now good practice with public appointments, or governorships at schools and colleges, that they are only for a limited period. That provides an effective discipline of stopping doing things.

Stopping things not only has a benefit for us, it has a benefit for others of giving them opportunities. With adequate notice stopping doing something is not letting people down but enabling others to have the opportunity. If no one wants to take on the responsibility there must be a question mark about whether the overall activity is worthwhile.

Key questions about what to stop doing are:

- Where do I add least value?
- What would be the consequences of stopping doing certain things?
- How can I best enable people to take on those tasks?
- What would be the benefits for me, in terms of release of time, of not doing certain activities?
- In the areas where I add least value, how can I best withdraw?

- How can I best nurture people to be able to take on these responsibilities?

Keeping vitality when your career has peaked

Keeping up energy is easiest when there is another hill to climb which you recognise is attainable. It is a very different experience when the hill is certainly out of reach or your capacity to climb hills is not as strong as it was. We tend to live in the day-to-day when we think that the energy levels we currently have will always stay with us. We don't prepare ourselves very effectively for when our energy levels change.

For each of us there is a point when we sense our career has peaked. To many people our individual plateau might seem like an unattainable mountain. When you plateau key needs are:

- to be very positive about what has been achieved,
- to reflect on how your skills and competences can be used in other ways,
- to gain considerable pleasure out of mentoring others, and
- to see how you can contribute in ways that enable others to do well and fly.

There can be very depressing moments when you know you are not going to become a head of department, a senior executive or a director general. But it can be a positive moment too when you say 'I am not going to climb this greasy pole any more and I am going to use my talents to the best possible effect in the role I currently have or a new role'. These defining moments can bring a new freshness when there is a self-awareness that what you enjoy most is teaching in the classroom, working as a probation officer with individual young people, working with community groups as a police superintendent or mentoring others to develop their skills in accounts management.

Part of the preparation for when your career peaks is necessary when you are still climbing the greasy pole. Keeping up current interests, intellectual, physical, emotional and spiritual, means that when your career peaks there are a wealth of other things that engage you that you can take forward. Avoiding the splendid isolation of being a one-dimensional person purely concerned with work is crucial in preparing for those moments when your career has plateaued or the employer decides he no longer needs you. These moments will come: it is only a matter of when. It is so easy to avoid preparation but so valuable to prepare effectively.

Allowing blank space

Vitality is not always about doing things. Often it is about just having space and not filling it. Michael is a very energetic CEO. He plans his working day meticulously. He is admired for the way no minute is wasted and every contribution has a specific purpose. He is a model of time management. Events are planned meticulously and run like clockwork. He times his interventions in meetings to perfection.

At the weekend he says that his greatest joy is doing nothing in a planned way. He says it is great to have a blank diary. He likes to be able to decide with his wife on a Saturday morning what they want to do. It might be a cycle ride or redoing the kitchen. It might be resting. What gives him energy at the weekend is being in the country and breathing in the air and doing something different. His energy comes from being completely detached from the office. He lives in the Pennines, far away from where he works. In the office he is energised by people, conversation and powerful purpose. Structure and clarity are vital in the office; outside, it is the absence of structure that provides him with the energy he needs.

Doing nothing and then doing something spontaneous is not a waste of time. When you are driven to succeed the idea of doing nothing for an hour or two seems futile. But maybe that space of emptiness is crucial for our wellbeing as we prepare for our next steps.

Janet describes a similar pattern to Michael. When she held a senior position in a finance institution her energy at work came from helping other people learn, watching the light go on as they decided on a particular course of action. She talked to people in the morning and tried to do the written work in an afternoon when she was most creative. She was determined to make progress in her jobs and always ensured effective change happened.

Her energy outside the office came from good friendships. She was fully herself with her friends sharing love and trust. She relished sharing ideas and a sense of humour with them. With friends she could cast off the mask and be completely relaxed. The best context was over a meal, be it in the kitchen or in a restaurant. Creating a convivial atmosphere was so important in creating relaxation. Her moments of peace and emptiness came from long baths with a book. Cooking was a powerful relaxer, especially when she was chopping things and putting different ingredients together.

Perhaps her most surprising way of finding quietness was knitting. She found it completely absorbing. The physical routine helped give her calmness and rhythm. She often did it on the train going to work as a means of settling herself before entering the hectic activity that was her working day. If she needed to relax on the train it was doing the knitting; if she wanted to reflect in a different way it was reading a book, because curiosity and learning was her biggest energiser.

It is worth reflecting on:

- What sort of blank space do you enjoy most?
- When can you do absolutely nothing?
- Do you create enough time to do absolutely nothing?
- How ready are you just to stand and stare?
- What are your plans for times in the future when you can enjoy blank space?

When your vitality goes completely

There may be moments when your vitality goes completely. The effect of a long busy period can completely sap your energy. Maybe you went down with a heavy cold or pneumonia and returned to work too quickly. Maybe you keep pushing yourself very hard. You have overcome a heavy cold before so you can do it again!

Sometimes it is very important that we listen to our bodies and stop. When we are completely exhausted we need to take the drastic decision of stopping and cancelling all engagements for a few days. A very robust decision to stop and cancel meetings and 'rest' for a while is not an acknowledgement of weakness, it is being realistic about the fact that your body and mind need to turn off. It would be madness not to listen to your body.

We can all be ridiculously macho when, for our own good, we need to take a break. Your complete lack of physical and mental energy may feel like falling into a black hole. Sometimes a restful weekend is all that is needed to climb out of the hole; on other occasions it might be a long haul. If the exhaustion is gripping, you are not the first to travel down that road. Never be too proud to seek medical help.

If your vitality goes completely reflect on:

- What are the likely causes?
- How can you best rest?
- What is the worst that could happen if you took a complete break?
- How long a break might you take?
- What is the best form of refreshment and renewal for you?

Vitality and the use of personal finance

When money is tight vitality is sapped. After my father died there was very little money available and not much opportunity for new or different things. Vitality came through playing football and cricket in the local park rather than going on holiday.

It is worth checking yourself as to how much store you are setting by material wellbeing. But there is an inverse pride that can take over too. We had our family car for sixteen years and took great pride about not spending money on a new car, when we could have afforded one. Sometimes not spending money can be a good source of vitality!

It is also worth thinking about what is the right link for you between where you spend money and vitality. Giving away money to a worthwhile charity is likely to provide you with a special source of new energy. Restoring an old piece of furniture rather than buying a new one might give you great pride. Investing money in books might be a great source of new ideas: if so, never begrudge the expenditure.

It is worth reflecting on:

- How much money do you really need to live on?
- Could you live in a more financially responsible and environmentally friendly way?
- Could you increase your giving to charitable organisations you support?
- What is the link between your levels of giving and your sense of wellbeing?

Moving on

Sometimes we are immersed in the present. On other occasions we are dreaming dreams. For each of us there will be a time to move on from what we enjoy or what has given us our livelihood. It can be painful to leave friends and work we have enjoyed. It can also be a huge release and a source of considerable new energy.

After over thirty years working in Government I had mixed feelings about moving on. I wanted to move into a different sphere but felt a great loyalty and affection for the Government Department which had been my home. Within four days of leaving, my previous work seemed like ancient history. The transition into a new world was what I wanted but was apprehensive about. It was such a joy to then be doing coaching work on a regular basis rather than just as a part-time activity. Moving on for me created a whole new energy.

Moving on is about thinking through:

- Where would you like to be in the future?
- What are the talents you would particularly like to draw on and which would give you the greatest joy?
- What contribution would you like to make to the community you live in?
- How can moving on be an opportunity to balance your time and energy in a very different sort of way?
- What have you not done that you would love to do, that could be part of the next phase?

Linking energy and personal happiness

Suma Chakrabarti talks of his early days professionally when his own success energised him. He liked to be different: he got a great buzz out of a succession of very demanding jobs which he did well.

His sources of energy have now changed. He says that what gives him greatest energy now is bringing people on. He has seen a number of people develop their skills effectively as a result of his mentoring which gives him immense joy. As he gets older (he is still in his forties) exercise is important. When he feels fit he feels more positive at work. When there is a lot of buzz about his friendship with his daughter, it rubs off into his enjoyment of work. He works very hard in the week but stops on a Friday night and only starts up again on Sunday evening.

Suma links energy and happiness. He says that what makes him happy is to smile, being positive about the future and being clear about his contribution helping to alleviate poverty. He admits it is very difficult to divorce personal feelings from his levels of vitality at work. His advice is 'Do not forget to maximise whatever energises you. Don't underplay the importance of recognising what makes you happiest and reinforce that in the way you use your energy.'

Possible reflections on vitality are:

- Are you clear about what gives you greatest energy?
- How can you best take steps to maximise the effective use of your energy at work?
- How can you grow those interests outside the office which help you develop your energy most effectively?
- What incentives work most effectively for you in terms of focusing and rewarding your vitality?
- When your energy levels are low do you give yourself enough space and legitimacy to do absolutely nothing?
- Can you nurture relationships with those colleagues and friends who best energise you?

Chapter 6:

Courage and Calmness

'I'm brave generally', *he went on in a low voice: 'only today I* *happen to have a headache'*.

Lewis Carroll

Courage and calmness are the forces that keep the 4 Vs in equilibrium. Courage comes from the inner resources which enable you to make a difference in a situation of conflict. Calmness is about a purpose and peace of mind that takes you through difficult situations. Both qualities are reflective and bold at the same time.

Focusing on vision, values, value-added and vitality is meaningless without courage and calmness.

- Living your **values** requires a conviction that those values are important with the courage to turn those values into
- a **vision** which is bold and yet one you are reasonably comfortable with in your calmest moments (not too comfortable with or the vision may be too easy). To achieve that vision
- the **value-added** needs to be courageous in its focus and its intent with a calmness that comes from being single-minded.
- The necessary **vitality** results from the courage to do a range of different things and a calmness that enables you to enjoy a range of activities that feed and reinforce one into another.

Courage

Courage takes many different forms. In an interview for the *Sunday Times Magazine* (5 June 2005) Barry McGuigan and his daughter Danika talked of each other's courage. Barry won the WBA World Feather-weight title in 1985. He was an impressive champion who gained great respect for his courage in the boxing ring. Eight years ago, finding out that his 11-year-old daughter Danika had leukaemia was like being hit with a sledgehammer. He said that no amount of fighting in the ring could have prepared him for it; this courageous boxer was terrified. They had to perform an emergency tracheotomy which involved putting a hole in Danika's neck. Barry had always considered himself one of those people who could deal with the problems life threw at him, but when this happened he felt completely emasculated: 'It was like our roles were reversed: this time it was my little girl who was the fighter. All I could do was sit and watch. And God, did she fight.' After a year and a half she began to turn the corner and asserted 'Daddy, I will never ever get sick again'. She did not look back and found a love of drama. The effect of the illness is that for this 'dynamo' girl the glass is never half-empty and never half-full: it is completely full.

Danika describes her father in these words: 'What I admire about Dad is his determination. If he decides he is going to do something he does it. When he was preparing mentally for his fights he would say "You could train all day in boxing, but if you don't have the right mental attitude you might stay standing half a round but you were never going to win a fight".' Danika said that her Father used to repeat 'Tough times don't last, but tough people do' or 'It's not the size of the dog in the fight, but the size of the fight in the dog'. The courage of the father had transferred to the daughter. For the father it was courage in the boxing ring, for the daughter it was courage to fight through leukaemia. That sense of courage was transferred into a very different sphere.

It is well worth reflecting on:

- Where does your sense of courage come from? Is it from a parent, a role model or particular experiences?
- When is your courage at its strongest?
- How can you best harness your courage for good?
- In what type of situation does your courage let you down?
- How can you prepare for those situations so that you maintain your courage?

Courage does not come from a bloated sense of your own importance or a quick burst of whisky. Courage is something much more deep-seated, about:

- having a clear vision of what you want to achieve,
- being comfortable with your values,
- conquering fear,
- being willing to be bold when you feel strongly about an issue,
- knowing what happens if you are courageous in terms of how you feel and how you cope, and
- recognising and enjoying the courage of others and learning from their approaches.

Actively strengthening your gift of courage can be such a worthwhile investment. If your quota of courage is enhanced you will keep going more effectively in difficult situations. You will be less daunted by crises and less likely to wake at 4 a.m. Different ways of developing courage might be:

- Recognising your own weaknesses and trying different ways of overcoming them.
- Observing people you regard as courageous and seeing how they demonstrate that boldness in a way that works.
- Talking with people who have shown courage in a whole range of different situations – that might be in sport, in community activities or in overcoming health problems.
- Identifying two or three aspects of courage in people you admire which you want to embrace and embedding those aspects of their courage in your decisions.
- Observing people of different ages – watch a youngster and their persistence in trying to do a task, or reflect on the life of an elderly person and the courage they have shown through hardship or illness.

Courage is infinitely transferable from one world into another. When we admire the courage of somebody in one sphere we can embrace something of that courage in the activities in which we are engaged.

Sustaining that courage depends on a clear conviction that what we are trying to do will make a difference. Making a difference extends from helping to alleviate world poverty to defusing a domestic situation or doing well in a golf tournament. The courage to make a difference in one sphere will affect the way we are able to make a difference in another sphere.

Beverley Stone in *The Inner Warrior* argues that all the theory about change or training is irrelevant if courage is missing. Courage is a necessary component of all change. Included within her components are the courage to:

- be unafraid to express yourself, and
- challenge assumptions, be innovative, take risks and try out new ways of doing things, confront vested interests, win over the sceptics, and disagree openly and honestly.

She talks of each individual having their own 'Inner Warrior'. This Inner Warrior is the source from which we derive the courage and the will to act in accordance with our values, attitudes and beliefs. She says it is a philosophy of life that encompasses your vision of how you want the world to be with an understanding that change will not happen unless you, as an individual, act. She links courage with compassion. She argues that without courage individuals can be resentful, disillusioned, underachieving, guilty and disconnected. Courage enables them to not tolerate game playing, to effect changes, and to be proactive colleagues and be fulfilled. She talks of the courage to stop conversations that are destructive.

Part of courage comes from learning lessons from hardship. Hardships both come from our backgrounds and can be deliberately self-inflicted (e.g. camping in pouring rain). Ross Moxley and Mary Lynn Pulley in their chapter on 'Hardships' in *The Center for Creative Leadership Handbook of Leadership Development* talk about painful experiences that lead to self-knowledge leading to personal reflection. People easily get caught in an endless cycle of repetition relying on the habits they developed yesterday to deal with the challenges they face today and will face tomorrow. Moxley and Pulley's belief is that with reflection and appropriate support, individuals can develop new levels of self-clarity from hardships and therefore provide themselves with a resilience necessary for survival.

You might reflect on:

- What hardships have you faced?
- How have they influenced the way you approach specific issues?
- How well will you cope with future hardships?

Courage is also about the courage to wait. The best next step may be to do nothing. When all around are demanding action the most difficult choice may be to wait. This is not lack of action through indecision, but placing importance on reflection and the right timing of decisions.

Calmness

Calmness comes in many different shapes and sizes. It is the moment:

- the child falls asleep in your arms,
- the minute after a dramatic piece of music ends on a CD,
- the peaceful moment looking at the still blue water of a sheltered lake,
- the few moments before you fall into a deep sleep,
- the quiet assurance when a good piece of work has been completed, or
- the occasions when your son or daughter gives you a hug.

We all need our treasured moments of calmness to help sustain us through ever busy days. Whether the hectic nature of your life is:

- never-ending phone calls,
- 150 emails a day,
- demanding and unruly children,
- surly or impatient customers, or
- our own children, full of mischief and unguided energy, finding your own form of calmness is so important in these situations.

It can be helped so much by:

- having a favourite photograph on your desk,
- recalling in your mind a calm scene or peaceful piece of music,
- having brief conversations with someone you love who has the effect of calming your fears,
- reflecting on a piece of poetry you know well,
- recognising the bond between you and other people in similar situations,
- enjoying whatever form of spiritual reality is important to you,
- not being too shy about admitting your own apprehension to others,
- allowing yourself to believe that inner peace and calm is attainable, or
- allowing yourself to be fully loved by those most important to you.

Calmness can sometimes come at unexpected moments. Often in crises there can be moments of calm which put a complex situation into perspective. In his autobiography, *A Lifetime in a Race*, Matthew Pinsent tells the story of the Olympic Final in 2000 when the Great Britain and Italian crews were neck and neck. He writes about them moving rapidly to the finishing line:

> 'My heart is racing, maybe up at 190 beats a minute. It's as severe a test as I have been through in years. It is all pain from the neck down, muscles driving, stretching, reaching and working. But there is a pocket of calm inside, a mental calculation that is ticking over, ready to send out more commands. Another gear maybe, but the legs are not happy about it. More importantly, it tells me I'm OK, I'm in charge, this is going to be fine.'

The special picture is of a 'pocket of calm inside' in the most tense and demanding of situations. Maybe sometimes we have to create our own pocket of calm and then nurture it. Peter Senge and his co-writers of *The Fifth Discipline Fieldbook* talk of the importance of moments of awareness when we pause and ask ourselves:

- What is happening right now?
- What do I want right now?
- What am I doing right now to prevent myself from reaching that outcome?

and then take a deep breath and live on.

There are various books on the market aiming to help build calmness. For example, the authors of *The Mind Gym: Wake Your Mind Up* have produced a very practical guide which talks of the importance of tranquillity coming through visualising coping successfully with any situation. Many of the books reflect on the value of:

- building rhythms into daily lives,
- celebrating what has worked well,
- bringing into play all your senses,
- finding means of escape for a while (either physically, mentally or emotionally),
- standing back and seeing the bigger picture, and
- enjoying the friends around you and indulging in their company.

Linking courage and calmness together

The most fulfilled of people link together courage and calmness. For example Mary is a highly successful operations director for a national organisation. She says that her courage is at its strongest when she sees the outcomes to which she is working. Once she has delivered the outcomes the commitment and the courage can sap away. That is the point when she needs to move on to find a new set of outcomes which will mean that her courage batteries are fully recharged. She has a strong self-awareness about the circumstances in which she feels courageous and the circumstances when she is likely to feel bored or disengaged. That self-awareness has been crucial to her success.

Mary had been the driving force setting a vision for major changes in an area of policy. She had learnt that to make a difference was not about changing her personality, it was using her single-mindedness to set a clear vision and be a driving force. She is a quiet, reflective person. Her courage is not expressed in grand speeches but in getting alongside key individuals and building agreement about next steps. She summed up her courage as never being afraid of different people or different situations. Her approach was always to understand where people are coming from and then to have the courage of her convictions to set out what she believed to be the right course of action. Her mantra was 'listen to the questions, understand the concerns and do not be browbeaten into submission'.

Mary's approach is to never assume that things will be all right in the end, even if the direction is sound. Her intention is to keep focus on all the key people being energised and to keep ensuring there is agreement that the outcomes are right, while remembering that it is worth the hard work of building up the goodwill of others as it is easy to lose it if you take them for granted. Her courage is based on relentlessly building up key relationships and building a common mind about next steps. Her success as a senior manager is based on never being afraid to give hard messages but always to do it with courtesy and kindness.

For Mary, calmness is part of courage. She is teaching herself to breathe more deeply and sometimes slow down the pace with which she says things. Sometimes the courage within her wanted her to push her conclusions quickly. She recognises that what is often needed is to take people through the next steps a little more slowly to enable them to come on board with what she is saying. She needs that deep breathing to give the calmness in order to be taking the next steps in the right sort of measured way. Because she is relatively small she is conscious that she can come over as not having a lot of gravitas. She does not want to come over as aggressive and domineering but does want people to take her views seriously and listen to them carefully.

Developing a sense of presence and impact for Mary is partially about having the courage of her convictions but also bringing a measured calmness so that she speaks authoritatively and ensures she has people's attention without making them defensive or unsettled.

There is a danger that we are too proud in not admitting our weaknesses. The more honest we are about our own strengths and failings the more we can define the nature of courage that is most important to us and the forms of calmness that will best help us live the vision that we want to live. Without courage and calmness:

- our vision will become either unattainable or deeply worrying,
- our values will become a burden and not a joy,
- our sense of value added will be ill-focused and depressing, and
- our vitality will be volatile and unpredictable.

Some final thoughts:

- What are your sources of courage and when do you feel most courageous?
- What are your sources of calmness and when are you at your most calm?
- In what aspect of your life do you want to develop your courage more?
- How can that developing courage be transferred into other aspects of your life?
- How can you develop greater depths of calmness in terms of your physical, emotional and spiritual wellbeing?

Chapter 7:

What is Success?

In all things, success depends upon previous preparation, and without such preparation there is sure to be failure.

Confucius

Success comes in many different shapes and sizes. Success for a 12-month-old child is the first step: this success brings pleasure to parents and, especially, grandparents. Success for the 94-year-old may be getting through a day without becoming totally exhausted: it may be remembering the names of people and not feeling too foolish.

Success is both in the eye of the individual and the beholder. Sometimes we feel a complete failure when others think we are an overwhelming success. Sometimes what we regard as significant minor successes are seen as irrelevancies by busy people around us.

Helping to deliver outcomes or be part of successful outcomes is an important driver. We delude ourselves if we pretend that we are not interested in outcomes. That very dismissal of being interested in outcomes means that we are defining what is important to us – that is, the absence of seeking specific outcomes.

Society needs driven people. Our economy needs people who are driven in terms of generating economic success. Our public services need people who are driven by the motivation to provide the best possible service to the public. Our schools need teachers who are committed to their pupils. Hospitals need people who are driven by their vocation of providing health care.

But being excessively driven can also be dangerous. We can be too single-minded for our own good. We can be blinkered to the impact we are having on others. A single-minded focus on one sort of success can be very damaging to people caught in the wake of this powerboat surge on focused outcomes.

Understanding our driven nature and being clear on how we want to focus that energy is essential if we are to succeed in the areas that are important to us. But if we are too blinkered we do not understand the nature of that success or its impact on others.

Success at work

What sort of achievement is most important to you at work? This is where being absolutely honest helps. Is it about:

- an income stream,
- status,
- influence,
- responsibility, or
- the outcomes you particularly want to achieve?

Often it will be a mixture of things. As a college lecturer, success is about the examination results and the personal development of your students. It is also about an income stream for your family, an adequate environment in which to work, recognition of your contribution and a status in the college and in society.

Each of these aspects of success is fine in proportion. But if it is all about money the job will become a drag. If it is all about status there will not be that flexibility to cope with the ups and downs of organisational life. If it is all about promotion dealing with the ups and downs of the views of senior managers will become a depressing ritual.

It might help to think about success at work in terms of:

- Have I done my best and achieved what I am capable of?
- How far have I been able to deliver the vision of what is important to me?
- How far have I been able to live my values?
- Have I been able to be clear about where I can add value and then been able to do so?
- Have I been able to maintain a reasonable level of vitality in my work?

Success in our family life

An important question is what success is in different aspects of our life. In our family life success may be:

- a partnership with another person that is warm-hearted and enriching,
- family life where the children feel loved and at home,
- friendships which are mutually reinforcing based on a shared respect and affection,
- a quality of interaction within our families that is lively and mutually reinforcing, and
- a bond of love that can survive crises.

In family life the focus is often on how the children are growing up. Too much of a focus on examination success can create a one-dimensional view of success and undermine a youngster growing in knowledge and understanding in other spheres. And yet without some focus on examination success the youngster can drift into obscurity, depression and drugs.

Success in our community life

We are all involved in some way in the community in which we live. At the very least this means co-existing with our neighbours. It might also be conversations at the school gate, sharing in activities for young people, voluntary work in a hospital, community activities based around membership of a faith community or participation in school or college life. What is achievement in these spheres? It is about:

- Making a difference if we are seriously involved in a community activity.
- Helping a mutual understanding of different views if there are conflicts within a community.
- Providing the glue which enables people of different opinions living in the same neighbourhood to rub alongside each other effectively.
- Sometimes helping to provide a focus on what success actually is and what can be achieved.

If we are busy in our work, success for us in the local community may be occasional participation and building up a limited number of friendships.

But are we ambitious enough? Even if our working lives are busy, involvement in a community can provide a breadth of understanding and interest. All experience of community life will give us a greater understanding of human nature which can easily feed back into the work context. Lessons we learn about how best to listen to people and influence them will feed straight back into how we can do our jobs most effectively.

The driver for involvement in community activities is partly about the self-interest of what we learn and how you as an individual can receive some personal satisfaction out of such involvement. There is a wider value of involvement in a local community in terms of giving benefit to others. The values that are important to us in our lives knock into our work, our families and our community activities. There is an obligation on us to try and find some way in which we can add value in the local community so that our vision for our contribution as citizens is holistic, covering not only our work and our families but also the local community.

It is worth reflecting on:

- How are you involved in the local community?
- What is the learning that has come through that experience?
- In what ways would you like to be involved further in community activities?
- What would members of your family most appreciate your being involved in within the community?
- What time can you commit to this and where can you add greatest value?
- What is the biggest difference you can make in the community?
- What is the personal learning you are particularly seeking which could come from a new phase of community involvement?

Success is not victory

Gloating is the worst sort of success. The self-aggrandisement of declaring victory is virtually always pride before a fall. Too much glorification of victory will mean the harder it is to build mutual respect and working together with the opponents of one day who may become the necessary allies of the next day. Success ought to be a cause of celebration, but never by belittling others. Success is a frame of mind of being able to make a difference in a constructive way. A colleague described success in these terms:

- Real success is as stated by others and not you.
- Real success is only seen in hindsight.
- Real success is when it becomes part of a person's history.
- Real success is doing something that stands the test of time.
- Real success is achieving something you thought impossible or others thought impossible for you.

It is not indulgent to reflect on:

- What do other people see as your successes?
- What have you done in your life that you are most proud of?
- Which successes demanded from you the greatest courage?
- Which of your successes were the true fulfilment of your values?
- Which of your successes gave you most continuing vitality?

Nor is it self-indulgent to have an accurate self-perception of what you have done that has made a difference and worked. Some of the most encouraging moments for me have been:

- The joy of seeing some of the people I have worked with as a coach reach senior influential positions.
- The long-term impact of some of the policies I have been involved in as a government servant (such as the transformation of certain parts of Newcastle or the success of different education and employment policies).
- The delight of seeing some young people grow into very capable adults having spent time with them as teenagers.
- The growth in confidence and individuality of my children.

Success at different phases of life

Success may be very different at different phases of your life. A rather dramatic example comes from the experience of Terry Yorath, who was a successful footballer. He captained Wales to the quarter finals of the 1976 European Championships. In the 1960s and 1970s he was a member of the very successful Leeds United side; he was also a successful manager of various club sides. He was devastated when his 15-year-old son, Daniel, his 'soul brother and best mate' collapsed and died in front of him from a rare heart condition during a kick-about in their back garden. (*Daily Telegraph*, June 2005)

Handling the grief was difficult. The easiest means of relief – drink – led to the breakdown of his marriage and to a horrendous accident in which a woman was knocked down when Yorath was three times over the alcohol limit. As required by his community service order, every Wednesday morning he would go to an equestrian centre and wait for the call to lead the horses round. He looked after disabled youngsters and in between would muck out, enjoying the hard work of making a dung pile. Taking satisfaction from the efficiency with spade and manure seemed very distant from career achievements in the macho world of football, but his community service enabled a new phase of life to begin. There was an opportunity for a different form of success as he needed leading out of a period in which he had been unable to look forward in life. Terry Yorath found the start of a new form of success in serving others through the community service. He admits:

'In the last fourteen years I've dwelt on the past instead of look-ing ahead. I suppose I'm one of those people whose glass is always half-empty. I'd like that to change. The only way it will change is if I do look forward. I know that.' (*Hard Man, Hard Knocks,* Terry Yorath)

The Terry Yorath story is a clear example of success being different at different phases of our life. His success at Elland Road was celebrated by tens of thousands. His success in overcoming the problem of drink is celebrated by him and his family. Both have involved an immense amount of courage in rather different ways.

How open are we to different types of success in different phases of our lives? Through whose eyes do we want success to be measured?

How do you want to be remembered?

It is a frequently used phrase that no one will say on their death bed that they wished they had spent more time at the office. That phrase is a bit too trite to be helpful. Spending time at work can provide a strong fulfilment. Those who are unemployed and want work certainly believe that work is an important part of fulfilment.

In our work situation we will want to be remembered for making a difference. The memory of us in a particular work situation will diminish amazingly quickly. In our community role it may last a little longer. In our family situation, for better or worse, our values will be imprinted on the members of the next generation, whether they like it or not. It is still worth asking some questions:

- How do I want to be remembered in the place I work?
- How do I want to be remembered in the community activities in which I participate?
- How do I want my family to be remembering me in fifty years time?

An honest answer to these questions will help us reflect on what success is.

Success across each aspect of our lives

If we start from the premise that our physical, intellectual, economic, emotional and spiritual wellbeing is important, it is worth looking at each of these spheres to see what sort of success is important to us.

- In the physical realm it will be about personal health and fitness.
- In the intellectual sphere it will be keeping our minds active and alert and continually learning new skills and experiences.
- In our economic world it will be providing for the family and having a home in which to live, with enough food and heat to keep us comfortable.
- In emotional terms it will be about our emotional health and well-being and our sense of happiness and fulfilment.
- In terms of spiritual wellbeing it will be about a sense of having a purpose in life and being able to live out the religious or philosophical faith and practice that is important to us.

The hard work of success

When watching successful athletes we are aware of all the hard work that has gone into their training and preparation. Effective preparation is essential for success in any realm:

- In the physical realm it is about regular brisk exercise.
- In the intellectual sphere it is about keeping our brains active.
- In our economic world it is about working purposefully.

- In emotional terms it is about enabling moments of joy and embracing them.
- In spiritual terms it is about the coherence between our beliefs and values and the way we live our lives.

Celebrating success

We embed success every time we celebrate. Reliving the moments of success is not indulgence but reinforcing our own worth. I can still remember the runs I scored playing cricket at school. I can still visualise the joy of standing on Saltburn Pier having walked across England from Arnside Pier. As a family we still remember with special pleasure the summer when we climbed Snowdon, Ben Nevis and Scafell Pike (the highest mountains in Wales, Scotland and England).

I encourage you to:

- visualise your moments of success,
- relive them regularly,
- articulate moments of success with friends and family, and
- be generous in your thoughts about those who helped ensure your success.

Often these occasions of success are defining moments for us in our life's journey. It is well worth both remembering those successful moments and reflecting on how they have influenced next steps on your journey. For example:

- How has a successful event at work influenced the next steps of your career?
- How has an enjoyable venture as a family helped to provide the bond which has been important at difficult times?
- How has a particular memory of good days helped you to keep going when sharing times with a family member suffering from ill health?

Richard, the CEO of an international organisation, gives this wise advice:

'Don't rush in to try and achieve just to make your mark. If you see a hole, don't feel you have got to fill it. Don't assume your perspective is always the right one. Pick up the signals from others. Be aware that to go quickly you may need to go slowly. Keep the pace right. Build up a clear understanding of the situation and your own reaction to it: be self-aware. When you are clear, but only then, define what success is important to you in making a difference. Then be absolutely honest about whether you are making a difference. Be clear about what making a difference every day means. Always think, would I want this particular achievement as my epitaph?'

Can I suggest that you reflect on:

- What sort of achievement really matters to you?
- How has that changed over time?
- How would you want your family to describe your success?
- What are the most important aspects of wholeness for you in terms of your physical, intellectual, economic, emotional and spiritual fitness and wellbeing?
- How do you want to be remembered in fifty years time?

Chapter 8:

Moving On

Fortune helps those who dare.

Virgil

This chapter is about the big picture, standing back and looking at your journey, where it came from and where it is going. I want to encourage you to reflect, against the background of the 4 Vs, on what sort of pilgrimage you are on. What are your guiding principles for the future and what are your next steps going to be?

Looking back

We think we change imperceptibly from month to month. Others will see dramatic changes. I often encourage people to reflect on how they have changed over a twelve-month period. Sometimes the changes are quite dramatic. Once an individual begins to gain in confidence and courage, their progress in terms of developing their leadership capabilities can be very rapid. If somebody gets stuck, then unless that road block is removed the journey seems to stop. It is very difficult to stand still, we are either going forwards or backwards: and when we are going backwards we often blind ourselves to that reality.

Perhaps once a year there is a strong case to cycle back in time and review how you have changed. The process should be conducted with an attitude of celebration and an acknowledgement of how far you have come. Do not cover over the problems and failures, but do not make them larger than they deserve to be. The point is not to say 'Look how I failed this year' or 'Look how successful I have been'. The point is to say simply 'Let me look at ... '

- How have I moved on in terms of my vision?
- How have my values been valuable in providing 'sticks in the ground'?
- In what ways have I added value most effectively?
- What have been the special moments of vitality?

The skill is then translating this backward reflection into looking ahead:

- What are the key elements of my future personal vision?
- How do I want my values to influence that vision and evolve?
- How do I want to develop my value-added in the future?
- Which are the new areas which are going to be sources of vitality?

The leader's journey

Moving on may well involve step changes in the way we behave. Stanton Marris, in their booklet 'Energising the Organisation: Holding On and Letting Go', talk of the leader's journey in the following way:

> 'The transition from control to leading through guiding principles is tough ... Most leaders will have risen to the top because of their ability to analyse, find solutions and persuade others. Not only is this behaviour reinforced in them by years of seeing it work, it is also expected by those around them. Now instead they are asked to find ways forward other than by analysis, by encouraging ideas and alternatives with which they may not agree and by trusting that people will work out within the spirit of the guiding principles.
>
> They are asked to cope with the paradox of letting go in order to hold on. In summary:
> Controlling leaders damage performance, the organisation and themselves,
> Enabling leaders energise people by freeing them to act within guiding principles,
> Guiding principles are drawn from what inspires people, not from the deliberations of a committee,
> To lead through guiding principles often requires a tough personal transition.'

A leader's journey is not just about life at work, it is about balancing a range of different priorities and preoccupations. However demanding or enjoyable the work environment is, keeping it in perspective is important. Being convinced that you want to work twelve hours a day, five days a week is fine, if it is something that is either a conscious choice or that you are prepared to live with, provided you are very much aware about its implications for other aspects of your life and for those 'significant others' in your life. A friend sent me the following reflection recently:

> 'Imagine life is a game in which you are juggling five balls. The balls are called work, family, health, friends and integrity, and you are keeping all of them in the air. One day you finally come to understand that work is a rubber ball. If you drop it, it will bounce back. The other four balls, family, health, friends and integrity, are made of glass. If you drop one of these it will be irrevocably scuffed, nicked and perhaps even shattered. And once you truly understand the lesson of the five balls you have the beginnings of balance in your life.'

This example is very visual. It is overstated to make a point, but is powerful nonetheless. One of the paradoxes is that the more we treat work as a rubber ball, the more we are likely to look at the situation we are in in a more detached way and be more ready to change and move on. We can become so fixated with a sense of loyalty to our work that we fail to see the bigger picture of where that particular work environment is going and whether our position within the organisation is becoming stronger or weaker.

What adjectives will describe you in five years time?

When you move into a new role or new organisation it is worth reflecting on the adjectives which you would want your new colleagues to use to describe you, and then to think about the behaviours and competences which will lead to those adjectives being an accurate description of who you are. It can be a worthwhile exercise to reflect on the adjectives that you want people to use about you in, say, five years time. It helps provide a framework about your learning and development over that period. I suggest as an illustration the following possible adjectives to describe your view of the future:

- bold
- responsive

- philosophic
- open-minded
- passionate
- generous.

Be bold

Some of the most enjoyable work I have done is about encouraging people to be bold in their thinking. It has been about:

- What impact would you really like to have?
- What sort of job do you think you are fitted for but have been hesitant to go for?
- What sort of influence would you like to have in your organisation?
- How can you best cut off from work pressures at the weekend?

Answers that are bold provide a basis for building personal confidence and resilience.

I have seen countless examples of where individuals have been bold in moving spheres and it has worked. Andrew was having a highly successful career within Government. He had moved every couple of years through a range of different jobs and built upon an excellent reputation for political understanding and influence. He wanted to be closer to delivery and was approached by a regional delivery organisation. After some apprehension he joined it, is thoroughly enjoying this new role and is pleasantly surprised how relevant his skills are. There are a wide range of issues on which he has been able to move thinking on because of his speed of mind, his clarity and his skill in building partnerships. There is a wonderful 'spring in his step'. The transition has been such a breath of fresh air for him.

Sometimes boldness does not work. The learning seems painful, but is powerful learning nonetheless. Most of us learn far more through our failures than our successes. The value of boldness is not only that we might succeed, but that the learning when we fail is enormous.

Be responsive

Expectations are changing dramatically all the time. Skills that worked well in one situation may well be outdated in a remarkably short period of time if we freeze them. Being responsive means:

- continually updating your technical competences,
- continually putting yourself in new situations so that your adaptability is constantly growing, and
- ensuring you push and challenge yourself to be ever more responsive alongside being true to yourself and drawing out your essential qualities of Wendy-ness, Mark-ness or Mohammed-ness.

Being responsive is about being up to speed in aiming to meet the competences that are particularly appreciated in the organisation in which you work. For example, the aspiring civil servant has to decide how they are going to respond to the focus the new Cabinet Secretary, Gus O'Donnell, is putting on pride, passion, pace and professionalism.

Within Accenture the aspiring senior executive has to decide how he or she is going to respond in the three main areas in which individuals are asked to perform, namely:

- a Value Creator who generates sustainable shareholder and stake-holder value,
- a People Developer, who creates a strong legacy and
- a Business Operator, who generates profits consistently in line with company targets.

Be philosophic

You can be the flavour of the month one day and completely out of favour the next. Your standing in any organisation depends so much on the expectations of the most senior leaders and whether your approach and style fits. You are only as good as your last success. All the hard work and achievement of the preceding years is as nothing if you are associated with a major failure whether or not it is your fault. This is a brutal fact of life.

If you do become linked with a particular failure caused by a third party your best option may well be to move out into another sphere. Of course it is often right to fight back if something of which you are part goes wrong. Reputations can be rebuilt, but often at an enormous price.

When you feel badly let down by someone who was previously your supporter and has turned into your critic, be philosophic. Your supporter who has become your critic may recognise what they have done although be highly reluctant to admit it: self-preservation is such a powerful driving force.

Be philosophic when things go wrong outside your control or you have been shafted or badly let down. Maybe it is all to the good, helping you move on to another place. Be just as philosophic when things go right. Maybe you have been the right person with the right approach at the right time. Yes, your skills have been recognised – celebrate that fact. Be very generous in spirit to those around you who were not as successful. The wheel can quickly turn full circle.

When you feel cross and want to 'kick the cat' know your own safety valve, be it exercise, conversation, meditation or watching an escapist film. And then try and turn the aggression into a search for the right next step where moving on will often prove a great blessing.

Be open-minded

To the extent that our wellbeing depends partly on thinking and doing new things, continuous experimentation is important to our mental and physical health. What are you going to do that is different?

- What new approaches can you experiment with in a work situation?
- How do you want to learn and grow in the work situation?
- What new people do you want to meet?
- How can existing friendships take on a new dimension?
- In what different ways can you maintain physical fitness?
- How can you stretch your understanding of the world?
- What wider reading can you enjoy doing?
- How can you understand more fully the emotional make-up of different people in your own and other cultures?
- How can your spiritual understanding grow so that it is not weighed down by the baggage of prejudice?
- What type of new ideas do you want to explore?

Deliberately seeking the freshness of new ideas and approaches is not indulgence. Possible next steps are:

- What are you going to do differently in terms of your daily and weekly routines?
- What new people do you want to meet and engage with?
- What cultures do you want to gain a better understanding of?
- How do you want to interrelate more effectively with people of a different faith understanding?

Be passionate

Bertrand Russell wrote in his autobiography: 'Three passions, simple but overwhelmingly strong, have governed my life: the longing for love, the search for knowledge and unbearable pity for the suffering of mankind.'

Are these the right areas to be passionate about? Being passionate about bonds of love with our family and friends is not soft indulgence. Being 'earnest in our affections' provides the bedrock of who we are. At the end of the day, maybe, 'Love is the only reality', for our family and friends will remember us long after our contribution at work has disappeared.

Bertrand Russell's passion for a 'search for knowledge' is central to our maintaining a positive outlook. Being passionate to learn and understand is such a driving force in terms of our moving on and growing all the time. Continuous learning is not something we just advocate for others, it is something that needs to be part of our being so that at the end of each year we can articulate how we have grown in knowledge, understanding and wisdom.

Perhaps more difficult is Bertrand Russell's passion of 'unbearable pity for the suffering of mankind'. His challenge is that our passion is not just observing distress it is doing something about it. We have such obvious possible opportunities such as giving a clear lead in terms of:

- fair trade: buying fair trade goods and advocating fair trade policies,
- climate change: in terms of restricting our use of external energy by action such as by walking, putting in solar panels and recycling whatever products we can, and
- community activities: through helping at a homeless shelter, visiting an old people's home or mentoring young people.

Having a passion about the 'unbearable pity for the suffering of mankind' can seem either irrelevant or overwhelming. For our own survival we have to put this passion in a wider context. But, as a leader, there is so much you could contribute that would both make a practical difference and help you fulfil your own passions.

Be generous

Some of the most influential people in my life have been those who have given generously of their time. These included Norman Anfield (the youth leader when I was a teenager), Hugh Jenkins (my first boss), Nick

Monck (the Deputy Secretary I worked for in the Treasury) and Jim Houston (the principal of the college I went to in Canada). In their different ways all of these people were generous with their time, their advice and their encouragement. They were quite tough on me too, but within the context of a very generous friendship.

You will undoubtedly have in your mind pictures of people who have been generous with you in terms of their time, support and encouragement. The biggest gift we can give to other people is to show that same generosity. Generosity includes:

- using your time in a focused way to help individuals keen to learn,
- thinking carefully about how we support and challenge individuals to enable them to grow effectively,
- providing a constant source of encouragement rooted in realism when we are talking with people about future opportunities, and
- always seeing the silver lining in every situation and helping people to move on from disaster.

People will sometimes take advantage of your generosity, and sometimes a return for your generosity can be many years coming. I met somebody recently who had eaten at our home twenty years earlier and then moved to another part of the country. He said he always remembered the hospitality and encouragement he received. It is this type of comment which can give special pleasure many years after the event.

Part of generosity is financial giving. Tithing is not such a silly idea. Sponsoring a charity that is important to you can bring rich rewards in terms of enabling others to make a difference for good. 'It is more blessed to give than to receive' is so true in every area of our lives. It is worth sometimes taking stock and asking if the time is right to be more generous with:

- your time,
- sharing your knowledge and understanding,
- providing support and encouragement,
- financial resources.

To be known for your 'generosity of spirit' is perhaps the most precious accolade you can be given.

Moving on – two examples

The following are two individuals who have moved on successfully. They have been bold, responsive, philosophic, open-minded, passionate and generous.

Georgina is a board member of a major national organisation. When she began her current job she lacked confidence, she was sometimes uncertain about the best way of making decisions and felt like a junior player. She had great qualities.

- She brought strong values into her role.
- She had a strong drive because of the way she was brought up: she was never half-hearted.
- She wanted to support people and help them grow. She wanted to enable people to do their jobs well so that they could look after their families effectively.
- She thought it important to take responsibility for mistakes and not point the finger at junior staff.
- She wanted to create an organisation in which each individual was respected, be that individual the CEO or the cleaner.
- Her passion was to create a society where there are more givers than takers.

Over the last twelve months she has grown markedly in confidence. She is now an influential member of the board: people seek her out because of her influential role. How has she changed?

- She is much more philosophic that she cannot change everything.
- She is more realistic in how she focuses her energy.
- She does not get knotted up about things she cannot alter.
- She observes herself more effectively and understands her impact on others.
- She has learned the value of different approaches, sometimes approaching issues directly and sometimes more circuitously.
- She recognises her maverick tendencies and uses them to good effect.
- She recognises that the job, however important, is 'only a job' which has meant that she is much more relaxed, reflective and therefore effective in what she does and says.

Georgina says that her values of loyalty, hard work and care for others are the same but the way she lives her values, and the way she adds value, has taken a step change. Her vision for the future is both more flexible and more robust. Her sources of vitality are still her husband, children and grandchildren.

Karen had a difficult boss. Her confidence had been completely sapped; her emotions were full of anger, resentment and fear. As we talked we worked through these emotions. One day I suggested that she might eventually view the boss as a 'gift' in terms of what she had learnt through the experience.

A few weeks later, after a lot of reassessment, Karen was focusing on applying for jobs. She was enjoying visioning what she could achieve in different roles. She was presenting her strengths capably. Soon she was appointed to a much more senior post than she had previously aspired to. Her vision, which had been previously shattered, was now reconstructed in a very different way. Her values had remained true in terms of her focus on making a difference and the ability to build successful teams. Her value-added had become more focused because of her rediscovered ability to make change happen. Her vitality, which had been dinted, was now so obvious for all to see. Karen had moved on dramatically within the space of two months. She could even see how the previous boss had indeed been a 'gift' because without that experience she would never have grown and moved on in the way she did.

Maybe you recognise from these two individuals some of the issues you have faced. Looking forward:

- Are you willing to be bold?
- How readily do you accept the needs to be responsive?
- How philosophic can you be when there are reverses?
- How open-minded are you to trying new approaches?
- How passionate are you about your next steps?
- How important is it for you to be generous?

Next steps

Is now a good time to take stock about how you want to take forward the 4 Vs? Maybe they can be a framework for your own leadership agenda. They can provide you with a self-assessment framework for the present that will continue to be relevant in the future. You could use the framework in a variety of different ways. For example, list under the 4 Vs:

- your current perspective,
- where you want to be in five years, and

● where you are now.

The framework can be particularly helpful when you apply for a new post. The illustrative case study in Annex 1 shows the relevance of the 4 Vs:

● before the crucial interview for a post,
● just before starting a job,
● three months into the role, and
● a year later.

The 4 Vs provide a framework relevant at each stage of the process of applying for and mastering a new job.

The framework can be equally applicable to a group. Annex 2 provides an illustrative framework for using the 4 Vs as a basis for a team deciding on next steps. The framework can be used effectively at any level and in any type of organisation.

My challenge to you, the reader, is to think hard about applying these 4 Vs. It might be helpful to write down your responses to the following questions:

● What is the **vision** of who you are that carries most resonance five years on? How do you want people to describe you, what are the adjectives you want people to use?
● What are the **values** that are most important to you now? What are the values that you want to be most important to you in five years time?
● What are the ways in which you want to bring a **value-added** contribution in your family, community and work worlds?
● What are your sources of **vitality** now and what sources of vitality do you want to grow?

Can you define your responses in each of these four areas? Perhaps it is something you could share with a colleague or friend. How might you then self-assess your progress in each of these areas? Who will hold you to account? How will you hold yourself to account?

My guarantee to you is that as you reflect on these 4 Vs and do some hard thinking about what are the right next steps for you, it will have a profound effect on your intellectual, physical, emotional and spiritual wellbeing. You might be more at peace with yourself. It will affect your economic wellbeing too. It might well make you poorer, but you will feel less uptight about your economic wellbeing.

Think of the legacy you want to leave behind. As you move on what will your colleagues remember of your vision, your values, your value-added and your vitality? How would you like to be remembered? How do you want to prepare the way so that you are remembered for positive aspects of the 4 Vs – that you lived by your values or you helped others grow their value-added? When you move on you will rapidly fade in their memories, but something for good or ill will stick in their minds: what do you want that legacy to be?

Think of the legacy you want to leave with your family. What will be your children's perspective on your vision, values, value-added and vitality? Will they treasure the memory or hide the pain? Amidst the balancing act of so many priorities we will leave an imprint on our families whether we like it or not!

What is the legacy we are giving ourselves? Every experience moulds us. Are we being moulded in the way we want? Are we enough in control of how our vision, values, value-added and vitality are being shaped? There will always be fixed points, especially our responsibilities to our families and our key values, but are we using the freedom we do have to have some impact on our own destiny and the legacy we want to leave behind?

Enjoy the journey of exploring the 4 Vs. It could well take you to some interesting and surprising places. I hope you come to see the 4 Vs as the corners of a precious diamond and that taken together the star they create lights up each dimension of your life.

Annex 1:

An Individual in a New Role: An Illustrative Case Study

This is a case study about an individual going for a promotion which shows the relevance of the 4 Vs at four stages:

- before the crucial interview,
- just before he started the new job,
- three months into the role, and
- a year later.

John had just been appointed to a senior level post. He was delighted as this was the culmination of years of hard work. There had been many disappointments. Sometimes he lost his confidence but there was an inner determination to reach a senior level.

Before the crucial interview

Various senior jobs came and went. He was often second or third in the interview process. The prize of promotion seemed elusive. Before the interview he worked on the 4 Vs.

- **Vision**. What would it be like to be inside the job? What would he be delivering? What would he be enjoying? He got so much inside the job in advance that when he went into the interview he could talk as if he was in the job, making a big difference.
- **Values**. He reflected on the values that were most important to him. How could he take forward those values in this job? What difference could he make for good? How could he so stretch and encourage people that they would welcome the leadership that he could bring?

Because there was a consistency between how he described his values and his vision, his perspective at interview was coherent and well thought through.

- **Value-Added**. Where would the job build on his strengths? What were the distinctive attributes he would bring to delivering this role better than anybody else? In aspects of the work that were new to him, how would his previous experience enable him to add value in a very distinctive way? In the interview he came over as authoritative and clear about his priorities and how he wanted to make an impact.
- **Vitality**. Why would this job energise him? How could he show that energy in an interview? Was he really going to be energised by this job or was it the thought of promotion or a change that was the incentive? Could he see himself continuing to be energised in the job even when it was tough? He gave a very powerful demonstration of a leader who would energise his staff well.

Working through the strands of vision, values, value-added and vitality meant that John went into the interview confident, composed and courageous. His joy when he got the job was contagious.

Just before starting the job

A few weeks later the story moved on. Just before he started the new job he explored these four strands again.

- **Vision**. What does his employer want him to deliver in six months time? What does he see as his key priorities? What is it most important for him to progress in the first hundred days? What are the key outcomes his employer is seeking?
- **Values**. How is he going to demonstrate the values that are most important to him? What will he say at the informal gathering for his senior staff in the first week? What are the key values he wants to get across? How does he want his colleagues to describe him to their friends? What is at the core of the values that he wants to be at the centre of his part of the organisation? He wanted to focus strongly on openness, honesty, frankness and effectiveness.
- **Value-Added**. Was he clear enough about where he is going to put his effort? He was conscious that he would need to prioritise hard and then prioritise again.
- **Vitality**. How is freshness and liveliness to be maintained? What could get in the way and how is he going to control the demons of sometimes

feeling low? How is he going to maintain his humanity in a tough introductory period? What are going to be his key sources of energy outside the office? Who is going to uphold him at a personal level in those first few weeks of a very tough new job? He was very clear about the time he wanted to spend with his family and the films he wanted to see.

Three months into the role

He entered the job confident and relaxed. The informal get-together with his senior staff followed by a thorough away-day went well. He felt he was making progress and becoming more relaxed. Three months in he looked at the same areas:

- **Vision**. What progress is being made by his organisation? Where they living up to his expectations? Were they being creative and energetic enough? Yes he was confident that good progress was being made.
- **Values**. Was he able to live his values? How were people describing him a few months into the job? Was he getting the right sort of feedback? Was he aware of contradictions or ambiguities? On the whole he was pleased with progress. He felt that he had been fair to his staff in the judgements he was making about them and also true to his boss in terms of ensuring a strong focus on effective delivery.
- **Value-Added**. Was he focused enough in where he was putting his effort? He as stretching himself, learning new skills and seeing some of the results of his innovations.
- **Vitality**. He was taking very little work home at weekends. He was working very hard during the week but he was enjoying the work, and the light at the end of the tunnel at the weekend was always an incentive. He did feel tired sometimes. Some of the pressures were unavoidable but he needed to do more to identify means of recharging his batteries.

A year later

A year later he was much more assured and confident. It had been a good year, following a steep learning curve. There had been crises along the way. But the direction of travel was strongly positive. Where was he a year on?

- **Vision**. There was a clarity about where he was taking his organisation. His initial vision had been shaped and modified through experience. He was now robust but could be flexible too. He had a clear vision of himself in the role that enabled him to be both purposeful and relaxed.
- **Values**. The same values of openness, honesty, frankness and effectiveness that he had shared at that first informal get-together with his staff are still what is most important to him. He has grown over the year but his core values are still rock solid. They had been tested by ups and downs but remained at the centre of his approach.
- **Value-Added**. He had kept prioritising. His boss had given him clear steers part way through the year. He was very grateful for her guidance which had helped to steer him. He was still learning new skills. Experience was a tough but worthy taskmaster.
- **Vitality**. He had kept up the energy. There had been moments when he had been drained but he had bounced back. He had managed to preserve his times to relax at the weekend. He had kept up the hockey. Playing the piano, although never skilfully, had been a crucial means of relaxing.

For John, the 4 Vs provided a valuable framework relevant at each stage of this process.

Annex 2:

A Team Deciding on Next Steps: An Illustrative Case Study

This annex looks at the applicability of the 4 Vs to a team deciding on next steps. The team could be in the public, private or voluntary sector. It could be dealing with an operational issue (such as implementing a new IT system) or it could be developing an approach to a particular problem (like designing a new hospital). The team could be either entirely self-contained or part of a much bigger organisation. The team might be relatively junior or the board of a major organisation.

The approach is based on asking members of the team to think through carefully key questions that relate to each of the 4 Vs.

Vision

Key issues for the team to consider would be:

- Is there a vision provided by an umbrella organisation which gives the framework for our work?
- How fixed is that vision and how much flexibility do we have within it?
- Is there a particular vision in the minds of the team's customers and partners?
- What is the right timescale to be looking ahead: is it two, three or five years?
- Are there any fixed points about what we as a team must deliver by a fixed deadline?
- How precise a vision do we need to have of what our outcomes are going to be: will flexibility be important?
- How will we know if we are making good progress?

- How adaptable is our vision to external circumstances?
- What are the biggest risks we are likely to face in reaching that vision: how prepared are we to deal with those risks?

Values

Key issues for the team are:

- Does the umbrella organisation have a clear set of values which are fully embedded?
- How best can we take forward those values and apply them in our work as a team?
- Are there particular values that are going to be particularly important to enable the team to succeed?
- What personal values do we bring to our work as individuals?
- What is the match between our personal values and the values that are going to be necessary to deliver the required outcomes?
- How robust are our shared values?
- What will happen if our values come under threat or scrutiny?
- What are the three most important values that we need to share as a team for us to be successful?
- How will we cope if there is a crisis? Will the values enable us to be resilient?

Value-added

The key considerations are:

- In what ways does the umbrella organisation expect the team to add value?
- What is the current match between the expectation of the umbrella organisation and what is delivered by the team?
- What is the overall value-added which we think we can bring as a team?
- What is the particular value-added as individual team members we want to bring?
- What is the combined effect of these different preferred value-added contributions: to what extent do they match what is needed in total?
- How might the preferred value-added of individual team members be modified in order to match the ideal for the team?

- What scope is there for training or coaching to enable individuals to develop the capacity to add value in a way that is most appropriate for the team?
- To what extent could team coaching help in ensuring that the value-added of each member adds up to the right overall contribution?
- Will defining the value-added to be brought by each member help build an overall picture about how the team is going to operate?
- How will we regularly monitor whether individual contributions are adding up effectively so that the overall total is more than the sum of the parts?

Vitality

Key issues to consider are:

- How energised is the team at present?
- How widely does the vitality level vary between different members of the team?
- At team meetings does the energy level rise or fall: what causes the energy level to change?
- What gives each member of the team most energy at work: how can that be built on by the team?
- What might the team experiment with in such areas as length, time and location of meetings in order to create variety and energy?
- What place does humour play in building vitality within the team?
- How creative is the team at the moment and in what sort of ways would it be valuable if the team could become more creative?

Methods of approach

Different ways of using the 4 Vs in a team could include:

- A self-assessment by each member which scores the team's strength under each of the 4 Vs on a scale from 0 (poor) to 5 (excellent). Each member could provide the scores and then there could be a discussion based on the overall results.
- An external facilitator could interview individuals and provide a summary report as a basis for discussion.
- The team could use the 4 Vs as a basis for an away-day using selective questions from the list above.

- A series of team meetings could look in turn at each of the 4 Vs.

Important ingredients are the willingness to be honest, open-minded, reflective and ready to be challenged and to challenge. Done honestly and frankly, working through the 4 Vs can provide a robust and purposeful way forward.

Annex 3:

Bibliography

Adair, J. (2003), *The Inspirational Leader*, London: Kogan Page.

Adair, J. (2005), *How to Grow Leaders*, London: Kogan Page.

Allan D., Kingdom, M., Murrin, K. and Rudkin, D. (1999), *?What If!: How to Start a Creative Revolution at Work*, Chichester: Capstone.

Anand, N. and Nicholson, N. (2004), *Change: How to Adapt and Transform a Business*, Norwich: Format.

Back, Philippa Foster, (2005), *Setting the Tone: Ethical Business Leadership*, London: Institute of Business Ethics.

Badaraccoo, J. (2002), *Leading Quietly: An Unorthodox Guide to Doing the Right Thing*, Harvard: Harvard Business School.

Bate, N. (2005), *Get a Life: Setting your Life Compass for Success*, Chichester: Capstone.

Bennis, W. and Goldsmith, J. (2003), *Learning to Lead*, Cambridge, MA: Perseus.

Bibb, S. and Kourdi, J. (2004), *Trust Matters: For Organisational and Personal Success*, London: Palgrave-Macmillan.

Blanchard, K. and O'Connor, M. (1997), *Managing by Values: How to Put Your Values into Action for Extraordinary Results*, San Francisco: Berrett-Koehler.

Bloch, B. (2005), 'You've Made a Mistake?', London: *Daily Telegraph*, 16 June.

Block, P. (1993), *Stewardship: Choosing Service Over Self-Interest*, San Francisco: Bennett-Koehler.

Bolchover, D. (2005), 'The Cricket Consultant: Duncan Fletcher', London: *Sunday Times*, 26 June.

Borg, J. (2004), *Persuasion: The Art of Influencing People*, Harlow: Pearson.

Bridges, W. (1980), *Transitions: Making Sense of Life's Changes*, Cambridge, MA: Perseus.

British Nuclear Group, (2005), *Business Profile*, Warrington: British Nuclear Group.

Cameron, E. and Green, M. (2004), *Making Sense of Change Management*, London: Kogan Page.

Cameron, K.S. and Quinn, R.E. (1999), *Diagnosing and Changing Organisational Culture: Based on the Competing Values Framework*, Harlow: Addison-Wesley.

Chadband, I. (2005), 'Cricket's Bullies Get a Taste of Their Own Medicine', London: *Evening Standard*, 21 July

Coffey, E. (2003), *10 Things That Keep CEOs Awake*, London: McGraw-Hill.

Covey, S.R. (1989), *The Seven Habits of Highly Effective People*, London: Simon and Schuster.

Department for Constitutional Affairs, (2005), *Making a Difference: Taking Forward our Priorities*, London: DCA.

Drucker, P. (2001), *The Essential Drucker*, Oxford: Butterworth-Heineman.

Drummond, N. (2004), *The Spirit of Success*, London: Hodder Mobius.

Edworthy, S. (2005), 'Yorath Takes the Lead from School of Hard Knocks', London: *Daily Telegraph*, June.

Erickson, J. (2004), *The Art of Persuasion*, London: Hodder and Stoughton.

Gladwell, M. (2000), *The Tipping Point*, London: Abacus.

Goleman, D. (2002), *The New Leaders*, London: Little Brown.

Grossman, W. (2005), 'How to Get it Without Leaving the Boardroom', London: *Daily Telegraph*, 16 June.

Handy, C. (1997), *The Hungry Spirit*, London: Arrow.

Higgins, R. (2005), 'Barry McGuigan and his Daughter, Danika', *Sunday Times* magazine, 5 June.

Highways Agency, (2005), *The Highways Agency Corporate Plan*, London: Highways Agency.

Holy Trinity Brompton, (2005), *Archbishops Lead the Cheers*, London: Holy Trinity Brompton.

Ind, N. and Watt, C. (2004), *Inspiration: Capturing the Creative Potential of your Organisation*, Basingstoke: Palgrave-Macmillan.

Kotter, J.P. (1995), *Leading Change: Why Transformation Efforts Fail*, Harvard: Harvard Business Review.

Maurik, J. van (2001), *Writers on Leadership*, London: Penguin.

Mind Gym, The (2005), *The Mind Gym: Wake your Mind Up*, London: Time Warner.

Morton, C. (2003), *By the Skin of Our Teeth: Creating Sustainable Organisations through People*, London: Middlesex University Press.

Moxley, R.S. and Pulley, M.L. (2001), 'Hardships', in *The Center for Creative Leadership Handbook of Leadership Development*, ed. C. McCauley and E. Van Velsor (2004), San Francisco: Jossey-Bass.

Nouwen, H.J.M. (1976), *Reaching Out*, London: Fount.

Owen H. (2000), *The Power of Spirit: How Organizations Transform*, San Francisco: Berrett-Koehler.

Pease, A. and B. (2004), *The Definitive Book of Body Language*, London: Orion.

Pinsent, M. (2004), *A Lifetime in a Race*, London: Random House.

Pulley, M.L. and Wakefield, M. (2001), *Building Resiliency: How to Thrive in Times of Change*, North Carolina: Center for Creative Leadership.

Rouse, R. (2005), 'Baroness Amos', London: *Evening Standard*, 21 July.

Russell, B. (1998), *Autobiography*, London: Routledge.

Sacks, J. (2000), *Celebrating Life*, London: Continuum.

Sacks, J. (2002), *The Dignity of Difference*, London: Continuum.

Sanborn, M. (2004), *The Fred Factor*, London: Random House.

Senge, P., Kleiner, A., Roberts, C., Russ, R., and Smith, B. (1994), *The Fifth Discipline Fieldbook*, San Francisco: Doubleday.

Shaw, P. A. (2004), *Mirroring Jesus as Leader*, Cambridge: Grove.

Shaw, P. A. (2005), *Conversation Matters: How to Engage Effectively with One Another*, London: Continuum.

Shepard, A. (2005), 'Nick Bollettieri', London: *The Times*, 25 June.

Sherwin, A. (2005), 'Big Brother is Christian Parable says TV Chief', London: *The Times*, 22 June.

Simms, J. (2005), 'Silent Protest', London: *Director Magazine*, July.

Stanton Marris, *Energising the Organisation*, London: Stanton Marris.

Issue 1	The Sources of Energy (2002)
Issue 2	Managing Energy (2002)
Issue 3	Leading with Energy (2003)
Issue 4	Managing the Energy (2002)
Issue 5	Decluttering (2003)
Issue 6	De-fogging (2004)
Issue 7	Holding On and Letting Go (2005)

Stone, B. (2004), *The Inner Warrior: Developing Courage for Personal and Organisational Change*, Basingstoke: Palgrave-Macmillan.

Thompson, P. and Graham, J. (2005), *A Woman's Place is in the Boardroom*, Basingstoke: Palgrave-Macmillan.

Wheatley, M.J. (2002), *Turning to One Another: Simple Conversations to Restore Hope in the Future*, San Francisco: Berrett-Koehler.

Wilkinson, M. (2005). 'Michael Cunnah', London: *Director Magazine*, July.

Wright, C. (2004), *The Business of Virtue*, London: SPCK.

Yorath, T. (2005), *Hard Man: Hard Knocks*, London: Celluloid.

Zohar, D. and Marshall, I. (2000), *Spiritual Leadership: The Ultimate Intelligence*, London: Bloomsbury.

Index

Index by Indexing Specialists (UK) Ltd.
Hove, East Sussex